FOREWORD

The collection of "Everything Will Be Okay" travel phrasebooks published by T&P Books is designed for people traveling abroad for tourism and business. The phrasebooks contain what matters most - the essentials for basic communication. This is an indispensable set of phrases to "survive" while abroad.

This phrasebook will help you in most cases where you need to ask something, get directions, find out how much something costs, etc. It can also resolve difficult communication situations where gestures just won't help.

This book contains a lot of phrases that have been grouped according to the most relevant topics. The edition also includes a small vocabulary that contains roughly 3,000 of the most frequently used words. Another section of the phrasebook provides a gastronomical dictionary that may help you order food at a restaurant or buy groceries at the store.

Take "Everything Will Be Okay" phrasebook with you on the road and you'll have an irreplaceable traveling companion who will help you find your way out of any situation and teach you to not fear speaking with foreigners.

TABLE OF CONTENTS

T&P Books Publishing

PRONUNCIATION

Letter	Russian example	T&P phonetic alphabet	English example
А, а	трава	[ɑ], [a]	bath, to pass
Е, е	перерыв	[e]	elm, medal
Ё, ё	ёлка	[jɔ:], [ɜ:]	yourself, girl
И, и	филин	[i], [i:]	feet, Peter
О, о	корова	[o], [o:]	floor, doctor
У, у	Тулуза	[u], [u:]	book, shoe
Э, э	эволюция	[ɛ]	man, bad
Ю, ю	трюм	[ju:], [ju]	cued, cute
Я, я	яблоко	[ja:], [æ:]	royal
Б, б	баобаб	[b]	baby, book
В, в	врач, вино	[v]	very, river
Г, г	глагол	[g]	game, gold
Д, д	дом, труд	[d]	day, doctor
Ж, ж	живот	[ʒ]	forge, pleasure
З, з	зоопарк	[z]	zebra, please
Й, й	йога	[j]	yes, New York
ой	стройка	[ɔi]	oil, boy, point
ай	край	[aj]	time, white
К, к	кино, сок	[k]	clock, kiss
Л, л	лопата	[l]	lace, people
М, м	март, сом	[m]	magic, milk
Н, н	небо	[n]	name, normal
П, п	папа	[p]	pencil, private
Р, р	урок, робот	[r]	rice, radio
С, с	собака	[s]	city, boss
Т, т	ток, стая	[t]	tourist, trip
Ф, ф	фарфор	[f]	face, food
Х, х	хобот, страх	[h]	home, have
Ц, ц	цапля	[ts]	cats, tsetse fly
Ч, ч	чемодан	[tʃ]	church, French
Ш, ш	шум, шашки	[ʃ]	machine, shark
Щ, щ	щенок	[ɕ]	sheep, shop
Ы, ы	рыба	[ɪ]	big, America

Letter	Russian example	T&P phonetic alphabet	English example
Ь, ь	дверь	[ʲ]	soft sign - no sound
нь	конь	[ɲ]	canyon, new
ль	соль	[ʎ]	daily, million
ть	статья	[t]	tune, student
Ъ, ъ	подъезд	[ʺ]	hard sign - no sound

LIST OF ABBREVIATIONS

English abbreviations

ab.	-	about
adj	-	adjective
adv	-	adverb
anim.	-	animate
as adj	-	attributive noun used as adjective
e.g.	-	for example
etc.	-	et cetera
fam.	-	familiar
fem.	-	feminine
form.	-	formal
inanim.	-	inanimate
masc.	-	masculine
math	-	mathematics
mil.	-	military
n	-	noun
pl	-	plural
pron.	-	pronoun
sb	-	somebody
sing.	-	singular
sth	-	something
v aux	-	auxiliary verb
vi	-	intransitive verb
vi, vt	-	intransitive, transitive verb
vt	-	transitive verb

Russian abbreviations

ж	-	feminine noun
ж мн	-	feminine plural
м	-	masculine noun
м мн	-	masculine plural
м, ж	-	masculine, feminine
мн	-	plural
с	-	neuter
с мн	-	neuter plural

T&P BOOKS

RUSSIAN
PHRASEBOOK

This section contains
important phrases that may
come in handy in various
real-life situations.
The phrasebook will help
you ask for directions, clarify
a price, buy tickets, and
order food at a restaurant

T&P Books Publishing

PHRASEBOOK
CONTENTS

T&P Books Publishing

The bare minimum

Excuse me, ...

Извините, ...
[izwi'nite, ...]

Hello.

Здравствуйте.
['zdrastvʊjte]

Thank you.

Спасибо.
[spa'sibə]

Good bye.

До свидания.
[da swi'danija]

Yes.

Да.
[da]

No.

Нет.
[net]

I don't know.

Я не знаю.
[ja ne 'znaʲʊ]

Where? | Where to? | When?

Где? | Куда? | Когда?
[gde? | kʊ'da? | kag'da?]

I need ...

Мне нужен ...
[mne 'nʊʒən ...]

I want ...

Я хочу ...
[ja ha'ʧu ...]

Do you have ...?

У вас есть ...?
[u vas estʲ ...?]

Is there a ... here?

Здесь есть ...?
[zdesʲ estʲ ...?]

May I ...?

Я могу ...?
[ja ma'gʊ ...?]

..., please (polite request)

пожалуйста
[pa'ʒaləstə]

I'm looking for ...

Я ищу ...
[ja i'ɕu ...]

restroom

туалет
[tʊa'let]

ATM

банкомат
[banka'mat]

pharmacy (drugstore)

аптеку
[ap'tekʊ]

hospital

больницу
[balʲ'niʦu]

police station

полицейский участок
[pali'ʦɛjskij u'ʧastək]

subway

метро
[met'rɔ]

taxi	**такси** [tak'si]
train station	**вокзал** [vak'zal]

My name is ...	**Меня зовут ...** [mi'ɲa za'vʊt ...]
What's your name?	**Как вас зовут?** [kak vas za'vʊt?]
Could you please help me?	**Помогите мне, пожалуйста.** [pama'gite mne, pa'ʒaləstə]
I've got a problem.	**У меня проблема.** [u me'ɲa prab'lema]
I don't feel well.	**Мне плохо.** [mne 'plɔhə]
Call an ambulance!	**Вызовите скорую!** [vɪzawite 'skɔrʊʲu!]
May I make a call?	**Могу я позвонить?** [ma'gʊ ja pazva'nitʲ?]

I'm sorry.	**Извините.** [izwi'nite]
You're welcome.	**Пожалуйста.** [pa'ʒaləstə]

I, me	**я** [ja]
you (inform.)	**ты** [tɪ]
he	**он** [ɔn]
she	**она** [a'na]
they (masc.)	**они** [a'ni]
they (fem.)	**они** [a'ni]
we	**мы** [mɪ]
you (pl)	**вы** [vɪ]
you (sg, form.)	**Вы** [vɪ]

ENTRANCE	**ВХОД** [vhɔt]
EXIT	**ВЫХОД** ['vɪhət]
OUT OF ORDER	**НЕ РАБОТАЕТ** [ne ra'bɔtaet]
CLOSED	**ЗАКРЫТО** [zak'rɪtə]

OPEN	**ОТКРЫТО** [atk'rɪtə]
FOR WOMEN	**ДЛЯ ЖЕНЩИН** [dʌa 'ʒɛnɕin]
FOR MEN	**ДЛЯ МУЖЧИН** [dʌa mʊ'ɕin]

Questions

Where?	**Где?** [gde?]
Where to?	**Куда?** [kʊˈda?]
Where from?	**Откуда?** [atˈkʊda?]
Why?	**Почему?** [patʃeˈmʊ?]
For what reason?	**Зачем?** [zaˈtʃem?]
When?	**Когда?** [kagˈda?]
How long?	**Как долго?** [kak ˈdɔlga?]
At what time?	**Во сколько?** [va ˈskɔlʲkə?]
How much?	**Сколько стоит?** [ˈskɔlʲkə ˈstɔit?]
Do you have …?	**У вас есть …?** [u vas estʲ …?]
Where is …?	**Где находится …?** [gde naˈhɔdɪtsa …?]
What time is it?	**Который час?** [kaˈtɔrɪj tʃas?]
May I make a call?	**Могу я позвонить?** [maˈgʊ ja pazvaˈnitʲ?]
Who's there?	**Кто там?** [ktɔ tam?]
Can I smoke here?	**Могу я здесь курить?** [maˈgʊ ja zdesʲ kʊˈritʲ?]
May I …?	**Я могу …?** [ja maˈgʊ …?]

Needs

I'd like ...	**Я бы хотел /хотела/ ...** [ja bɪ ha'tel /ha'tela/ ...]
I don't want ...	**Я не хочу ...** [ja ne ha'tʃu ...]
I'm thirsty.	**Я хочу пить.** [ja ha'tʃu pitʲ]
I want to sleep.	**Я хочу спать.** [ja ha'tʃu spatʲ]
I want ...	**Я хочу ...** [ja ha'tʃu ...]
to wash up	**умыться** [u'mɪtsa]
to brush my teeth	**почистить зубы** [pa'tʃistitʲ 'zubɪ]
to rest a while	**немного отдохнуть** [nem'nɔgə atdah'nʊtʲ]
to change my clothes	**переодеться** [perea'detsa]
to go back to the hotel	**вернуться в гостиницу** [wer'nʊtsa v gas'tinitsu]
to buy ...	**купить ...** [kʊ'pitʲ ...]
to go to ...	**съездить в ...** [sʰ'ezditʲ v ...]
to visit ...	**посетить ...** [pasi'titʲ ...]
to meet with ...	**встретиться с ...** [vstr'etitsa s ...]
to make a call	**позвонить** [pazva'nitʲ]
I'm tired.	**Я устал /устала/.** [ja us'tal /us'tala/]
We are tired.	**Мы устали.** [mɪ us'tali]
I'm cold.	**Мне холодно.** [mne 'hɔladnə]
I'm hot.	**Мне жарко.** [mne 'ʒarkə]
I'm OK.	**Мне нормально.** [mne nar'malʲnə]

I need to make a call.

Мне надо позвонить.
[mne 'nada pazva'nit']

I need to go to the restroom.

Мне надо в туалет.
[mne 'nada v tʊa'let]

I have to go.

Мне пора.
[mne pa'ra]

I have to go now.

Мне надо идти.
[mne 'nada it'ti]

Asking for directions

Excuse me, ...	**Извините, ...** [izwi'nite, ...]
Where is ...?	**Где находится ...?** [gde na'hɔditsa ...?]
Which way is ...?	**В каком направлении находится ...?** [v ka'kɔm naprav'lenii na'hɔditsa ...?]
Could you help me, please?	**Помогите мне, пожалуйста.** [pama'gite mne, pa'ʒaləstə]

I'm looking for ...	**Я ищу ...** [ja i'ɕu ...]
I'm looking for the exit.	**Я ищу выход.** [ja i'ɕu 'vɪhət]
I'm going to ...	**Я еду в ...** [ja 'edʊ v ...]
Am I going the right way to ...?	**Я правильно иду ...?** [ja 'prawilʲnə i'dʊ ...?]

Is it far?	**Это далеко?** ['ɛtə dale'kɔ?]
Can I get there on foot?	**Я дойду туда пешком?** [ja daj'dʊ tʊ'da peʃ'kɔm?]

Can you show me on the map?	**Покажите мне на карте, пожалуйста.** [paka'ʒite mne na 'karte, pa'ʒaləstə]
Show me where we are right now.	**Покажите, где мы сейчас.** [paka'ʒite, gde mɪ se'ʧas]

Here	**Здесь** [zdesʲ]
There	**Там** [tam]
This way	**Сюда** [sʲʊ'da]

Turn right.	**Поверните направо.** [pawer'nite nap'ravə]
Turn left.	**Поверните налево.** [pawer'nite na'levə]
first (second, third) turn	**первый (второй, третий) поворот** ['pervɪj (vta'rɔj, 'tretij) pava'rɔt]
to the right	**направо** [nap'ravə]

to the left

налево
[na'levə]

Go straight.

Идите прямо.
[i'dite 'prʲamə]

Signs

WELCOME!	**ДОБРО ПОЖАЛОВАТЬ!** [dab'rɔ pa'ʒalavətʲ!]
ENTRANCE	**ВХОД** [vhɔt]
EXIT	**ВЫХОД** ['vɪhət]
PUSH	**ОТ СЕБЯ** [at se'bʲa]
PULL	**НА СЕБЯ** [na se'bʲa]
OPEN	**ОТКРЫТО** [atk'rɪtə]
CLOSED	**ЗАКРЫТО** [zak'rɪtə]
FOR WOMEN	**ДЛЯ ЖЕНЩИН** [dʎa 'ʒɛnɕin]
FOR MEN	**ДЛЯ МУЖЧИН** [dʎa mʊ'ɕin]
MEN, GENTS	**МУЖСКОЙ ТУАЛЕТ** [mʊʃs'kɔj tʊa'let]
WOMEN, LADIES	**ЖЕНСКИЙ ТУАЛЕТ** [ʒɛnskij tʊa'let]
DISCOUNTS	**СКИДКИ** ['skitki]
SALE	**РАСПРОДАЖА** [raspra'daʒa]
FREE	**БЕСПЛАТНО** [bisp'latnə]
NEW!	**НОВИНКА!** [na'vinka!]
ATTENTION!	**ВНИМАНИЕ!** [vni'maniə!]
NO VACANCIES	**МЕСТ НЕТ** [mest 'net]
RESERVED	**ЗАРЕЗЕРВИРОВАНО** [zarizer'wiravanə]
ADMINISTRATION	**АДМИНИСТРАЦИЯ** [administ'raʦija]
STAFF ONLY	**ТОЛЬКО ДЛЯ ПЕРСОНАЛА** [tolʲkə dʎa persa'nala]

BEWARE OF THE DOG!	ЗЛАЯ СОБАКА
	['zlaja sa'baka]
NO SMOKING!	НЕ КУРИТЬ!
	[ne kʊ'ritʲ!]
DO NOT TOUCH!	РУКАМИ НЕ ТРОГАТЬ!
	[rʊ'kami ne 'trɔgatʲ!]
DANGEROUS	ОПАСНО
	[a'pasnə]
DANGER	ОПАСНОСТЬ
	[a'pasnəstʲ]
HIGH VOLTAGE	ВЫСОКОЕ НАПРЯЖЕНИЕ
	[vɪ'sɔkae napri'ʒɛnie]
NO SWIMMING!	КУПАТЬСЯ ЗАПРЕЩЕНО
	[kʊ'patsa zapriɕe'nɔ!]

OUT OF ORDER	НЕ РАБОТАЕТ
	[ne ra'botaet]
FLAMMABLE	ОГНЕОПАСНО
	[agnea'pasnə]
FORBIDDEN	ЗАПРЕЩЕНО
	[zapriɕe'nɔ]
NO TRESPASSING!	ПРОХОД ЗАПРЕЩЁН
	[pra'hɔt zapri'ɕ'on!]
WET PAINT	ОКРАШЕНО
	[ak'raʃenə]

CLOSED FOR RENOVATIONS	ЗАКРЫТО НА РЕМОНТ
	[zak'rɪtə na re'mɔnt]
WORKS AHEAD	РЕМОНТНЫЕ РАБОТЫ
	[re'mɔntnɪe ra'botɪ]
DETOUR	ОБЪЕЗД
	[abʰ'ezt]

Transportation. General phrases

plane	**самолёт** [sama'lʲot]
train	**поезд** ['pɔest]
bus	**автобус** [aft'ɔbʊs]
ferry	**паром** [pa'rɔm]
taxi	**такси** [tak'si]
car	**машина** [ma'ʃina]

schedule	**расписание** [raspi'sanie]
Where can I see the schedule?	**Где можно посмотреть расписание?** [gde 'mɔʒnə pasmat'retʲ raspi'sanie?]
workdays (weekdays)	**рабочие дни** [ra'bɔtʃiə dni]
weekends	**выходные дни** [vɪhad'nɪe dni]
holidays	**праздничные дни** ['prazdnitʃnɪe dni]

DEPARTURE	**ОТПРАВЛЕНИЕ** [atprav'lenie]
ARRIVAL	**ПРИБЫТИЕ** [pri'bɪtie]
DELAYED	**ЗАДЕРЖИВАЕТСЯ** [za'derʒivaetsa]
CANCELED	**ОТМЕНЕН** [atme'nʲon]

next (train, etc.)	**следующий** ['sledʊɕij]
first	**первый** ['pervɪj]
last	**последний** [pas'lednij]

When is the next …?	**Когда будет следующий …?** [kag'da 'bʊdet 'sledʊɕij …?]
When is the first …?	**Когда отходит первый …?** [kag'da at'hɔdit 'pervɪj …?]

When is the last ...?

Когда уходит последний ...?
[kag'da u'hɔdit pas'lednij ...?]

transfer (change of trains, etc.)

пересадка
[piri'satka]

to make a transfer

сделать пересадку
['sdelatʲ piri'satkʊ]

Do I need to make a transfer?

Мне нужно делать пересадку?
[mne 'nʊʒnə 'delatʲ piri'satkʊ?]

Buying tickets

Where can I buy tickets?	**Где можно купить билеты?** [gde 'moʒnə kʊ'pitʲ bi'letɪ?]
ticket	**билет** [bi'let]
to buy a ticket	**купить билет** [kʊ'pitʲ bi'let]
ticket price	**стоимость билета** [stɔiməstʲ bi'leta]

Where to?	**Куда?** [kʊ'da?]
To what station?	**До какой станции?** [dɔ ka'kɔj 'stantsii?]
I need ...	**Мне нужно ...** [mne 'nʊʒnə ...]
one ticket	**один билет** [a'din bi'let]
two tickets	**два билета** [dva bi'leta]
three tickets	**три билета** [tri bi'leta]

one-way	**в один конец** [v a'din ka'nets]
round-trip	**туда и обратно** [tʊ'da i ab'ratnə]
first class	**первый класс** ['pervɪj klass]
second class	**второй класс** [fta'rɔj klass]

today	**сегодня** [si'vɔdɲa]
tomorrow	**завтра** ['zaftra]
the day after tomorrow	**послезавтра** [pɔsle'zaftra]
in the morning	**утром** ['utrəm]
in the afternoon	**днём** [dnʲom]
in the evening	**вечером** ['wetʃerəm]

aisle seat

место у прохода
['mestə u pra'hɔda]

window seat

место у окна
['mestə u ak'na]

How much?

Сколько?
['skɔlʲkə?]

Can I pay by credit card?

Могу я заплатить карточкой?
[ma'gʊ ja zapla'titʲ 'kartətʃkəj?]

Bus

bus	**автобус** [aft'ɔbʊs]
intercity bus	**междугородний автобус** [meʒdʊga'rɔdnij aft'ɔbʊs]
bus stop	**автобусная остановка** [aft'ɔbʊsnaja asta'nɔfka]
Where's the nearest bus stop?	**Где ближайшая автобусная остановка?** [gde bli'ʒajʃeja aft'ɔbʊsnaja asta'nɔfka?]
number (bus ~, etc.)	**номер** ['nɔmer]
Which bus do I take to get to ...?	**Какой автобус идёт до ...?** [ka'kɔj aft'ɔbʊs i'dʲot dɔ ...?]
Does this bus go to ...?	**Этот автобус идёт до ...?** [ɛtət av'tɔbʊs i'dʲot dɔ ...?]
How frequent are the buses?	**Как часто ходят автобусы?** [kak 'tʃastə 'hɔdʲat aft'ɔbʊsɪ?]
every 15 minutes	**каждые 15 минут** ['kaʒdɪe pit'natsatʲ mi'nʊt]
every half hour	**каждые полчаса** ['kaʒdɪe pɔltʃa'sa]
every hour	**каждый час** ['kaʒdɪj tʃas]
several times a day	**несколько раз в день** ['neskalʲkə raz v denʲ]
... times a day	**... раз в день** [... raz v denʲ]
schedule	**расписание** [raspi'sanie]
Where can I see the schedule?	**Где можно посмотреть расписание?** [gde 'mɔʒnə pasmat'retʲ raspi'sanie?]
When is the next bus?	**Когда будет следующий автобус?** [kag'da 'bʊdet 'sledʊɕij aft'ɔbʊs?]
When is the first bus?	**Когда отходит первый автобус?** [kag'da at'hɔdit 'pervij aft'ɔbʊs?]
When is the last bus?	**Когда уходит последний автобус?** [kag'da u'hɔdit pas'lednij aft'ɔbʊs?]
stop	**остановка** [asta'nɔfka]

26

next stop

следующая остановка
['sleduɕeja asta'nɔfka]

last stop (terminus)

конечная остановка
[ka'netʃnəja asta'nɔfka]

Stop here, please.

Остановите здесь, пожалуйста.
[astana'wite zdesʲ, pa'ʒaləstə]

Excuse me, this is my stop.

Разрешите, это моя остановка.
[razre'ʃite, 'ɛtə ma'ja asta'nɔfka]

Train

train	**поезд** ['pɔest]
suburban train	**пригородный поезд** ['prigəradnɪj 'pɔest]
long-distance train	**поезд дальнего следования** ['pɔest 'dalʲnevə 'sledavanijə]
train station	**вокзал** [vak'zal]
Excuse me, where is the exit to the platform?	**Извините, где выход к поездам?** [izwi'nite, gde 'vɪhət k paez'dam?]
Does this train go to ...?	**Этот поезд идёт до ...?** [ɛtət 'pɔest i'dʲot dɔ ...?]
next train	**следующий поезд** ['sledʊçij 'pɔest]
When is the next train?	**Когда будет следующий поезд?** [kag'da 'bʊdet 'sledʊçij 'pɔest?]
Where can I see the schedule?	**Где можно посмотреть расписание?** [gde 'mɔʒnə pasmat'retʲ raspi'sanie?]
From which platform?	**С какой платформы?** [s ka'kɔj plat'fɔrmɪ?]
When does the train arrive in ...?	**Когда поезд прибывает в ...?** [kag'da 'pɔest pribɪ'vaet v ...?]
Please help me.	**Помогите мне, пожалуйста.** [pama'gite mne, pa'ʒaləstə]
I'm looking for my seat.	**Я ищу своё место.** [ja i'çu sva'ʲo 'mestə]
We're looking for our seats.	**Мы ищем наши места.** [mɪ 'içem 'naʃi mes'ta]
My seat is taken.	**Моё место занято.** [ma'ʲo 'mestə 'zaɲatə]
Our seats are taken.	**Наши места заняты.** ['naʃi mes'ta 'zaɲatɪ]
I'm sorry but this is my seat.	**Извините, пожалуйста, но это моё место.** [izwi'nite, pa'ʒaləstə, nɔ 'ɛtə ma'ʲo 'mestə]
Is this seat taken?	**Это место свободно?** [ɛtə 'mestə sva'bɔdnə?]
May I sit here?	**Могу я здесь сесть?** [ma'gʊ ja zdesʲ 'sestʲ?]

On the train. Dialogue (No ticket)

Ticket, please.
Ваш билет, пожалуйста.
[vaʃ bi'let, pa'ʒaləstə]

I don't have a ticket.
У меня нет билета.
[u me'ɲa net bi'leta]

I lost my ticket.
Я потерял /потеряла/ свой билет.
[ja pate'rʲal /pate'rʲala/ svɔj bi'let]

I forgot my ticket at home.
Я забыл /забыла/ билет дома.
[ja za'bɪl /za'bɪla/ bi'let 'dɔma]

You can buy a ticket from me.
Вы можете купить билет у меня.
[vɪ 'mɔʒɛte ku'pitʲ bi'let u me'ɲa]

You will also have to pay a fine.
Вам ещё придётся заплатить штраф.
[vam i'ɕʲo pri'dʲotsa zapla'titʲ 'ʃtraf]

Okay.
Хорошо.
[hara'ʃɔ]

Where are you going?
Куда вы едете?
[ku'da vɪ 'edete?]

I'm going to …
Я еду до …
[ja 'edu dɔ …]

How much? I don't understand.
Сколько? Я не понимаю.
['skɔlʲkə? ja ne pani'maʲʉ]

Write it down, please.
Напишите, пожалуйста.
[napi'ʃite, pa'ʒaləstə]

Okay. Can I pay with a credit card?
Хорошо. Могу я заплатить карточкой?
[hara'ʃɔ. ma'gu ja zapla'titʲ 'kartɛtʃkəj?]

Yes, you can.
Да, можете.
[da 'mɔʒɛte]

Here's your receipt.
Вот ваша квитанция.
[vɔt 'vaʃʌ kwi'tantsija]

Sorry about the fine.
Сожалею о штрафе.
[saʒe'leʲʉ ɔ 'ʃtrafe]

That's okay. It was my fault.
Это ничего. Это моя вина.
['ɛtə nitʃe'vɔ. 'ɛtə ma'ja wi'na]

Enjoy your trip.
Приятной вам поездки.
[pri'jatnəj vam pa'eztki]

Taxi

taxi	**такси** [tak'si]
taxi driver	**таксист** [tak'sist]
to catch a taxi	**поймать такси** [paj'matʲ tak'si]
taxi stand	**стоянка такси** [sta'janka tak'si]
Where can I get a taxi?	**Где я могу взять такси?** [gde ja ma'gu vzʲatʲ tak'si?]

to call a taxi	**вызвать такси** ['vɪzvatʲ tak'si]
I need a taxi.	**Мне нужно такси.** [mne 'nuʒnə tak'si]
Right now.	**Прямо сейчас.** ['prʲamə se'tʃas]
What is your address (location)?	**Ваш адрес?** [vaʃ 'adres?]
My address is ...	**Мой адрес ...** [mɔj 'adres ...]
Your destination?	**Куда вы поедете?** [ku'da vɪ pɔ'edete?]

Excuse me, ...	**Извините, ...** [izwi'nite, ...]
Are you available?	**Вы свободны?** [vɪ sva'bɔdnɪ?]
How much is it to get to ...?	**Сколько стоит доехать до ...?** ['skɔlʲkə 'stɔit da'ehatʲ dɔ ...?]
Do you know where it is?	**Вы знаете, где это?** [vɪ 'znaete, 'gde ɛtə?]
Airport, please.	**В аэропорт, пожалуйста.** [v aɛra'pɔrt, pa'ʒaləstə]
Stop here, please.	**Остановитесь здесь, пожалуйста.** [astana'witesʲ zdesʲ, pa'ʒaləstə]
It's not here.	**Это не здесь.** ['ɛtə ne zdesʲ]
This is the wrong address.	**Это неправильный адрес.** ['ɛtə nep'rawilʲnɪj 'adres]
Turn left.	**Сейчас налево.** [si'tʃas na'levə]
Turn right.	**Сейчас направо.** [si'tʃas nap'ravə]

How much do I owe you?	**Сколько я вам должен /должна/?** ['skolʲkə ja vam 'dɔlʒen /dɔlʒ'na/?]
I'd like a receipt, please.	**Дайте мне чек, пожалуйста.** [dajte mne 'tʃek, pa'ʒaləstə]
Keep the change.	**Сдачи не надо.** [sdatʃi ne 'nadə]

Would you please wait for me?	**Подождите меня, пожалуйста.** [padaʒ'dite me'ɲa, pa'ʒaləstə]
five minutes	**5 минут** [pʲatʲ mi'nut]
ten minutes	**10 минут** ['desʲatʲ mi'nut]
fifteen minutes	**15 минут** [pit'natsatʲ mi'nut]
twenty minutes	**20 минут** ['dvatsatʲ mi'nut]
half an hour	**полчаса** [poltʃa'sa]

Hotel

Hello.	**Здравствуйте.** ['zdrastvʊjte]
My name is ...	**Меня зовут ...** [mi'ɲa za'vʊt ...]
I have a reservation.	**Я резервировал /резервировала/ номер.** [ja rezer'virəval /rezer'virəvala/ 'nɔmer]

I need ...	**Мне нужен ...** [mne 'nʊʒən ...]
a single room	**одноместный номер** [ədna'mesnɪj 'nɔmer]
a double room	**двухместный номер** [dvʊh'mesnɪj 'nɔmer]
How much is that?	**Сколько он стоит?** ['skolʲkə ɔn 'stɔit?]
That's a bit expensive.	**Это немного дорого.** [ɛtə nem'nɔgə 'dɔragə]

Do you have any other options?	**У вас есть еще что-нибудь?** [u vas estʲ e'ɕʲo ʃtɔ ni'bʊtʲ?]
I'll take it.	**Я возьму его.** [ja vazʲ'mʊ e'vɔ]
I'll pay in cash.	**Я заплачу наличными.** [ja zapla'ʧu na'liʧnɪmi]

I've got a problem.	**У меня проблема.** [u me'ɲa prab'lema]
My ... is broken.	**Мой ... сломан /Моя ... сломана/** [mɔj ... 'sloman /ma'ja ... 'slɔmana/]
My ... is out of order.	**Мой /Моя/ ... не работает.** [mɔj /ma'ja/ ... ne ra'bɔtaet]
TV	**телевизор (м)** [tele'wizər]
air conditioning	**кондиционер (м)** [kəndiʦia'ner]
tap	**кран (м)** [kran]

shower	**душ (м)** [dʊʃ]
sink	**раковина (ж)** ['rakəwina]

safe	**сейф (м)** [sɛjf]
door lock	**замок (м)** [zaˈmɔk]
electrical outlet	**розетка (ж)** [raˈzetka]
hairdryer	**фен (м)** [fen]

I don't have …	**У меня нет …** [u meˈɲa net …]
water	**воды** [vaˈdɪ]
light	**света** [ˈsweta]
electricity	**электричества** [ɛlektˈriʧestva]

Can you give me …?	**Можете мне дать …?** [ˈmɔʒete mne datʲ …?]
a towel	**полотенце** [palaˈtentse]
a blanket	**одеяло** [adeˈjalə]
slippers	**тапочки** [ˈtapəʧki]
a robe	**халат** [haˈlat]
shampoo	**шампунь** [ʃʌmˈpʊnʲ]
soap	**мыло** [ˈmɪlə]

I'd like to change rooms.	**Я хотел бы /хотела бы/ поменять номер.** [ja haˈtel /haˈtela/ bɪ pameˈɲatʲ ˈnɔmer]
I can't find my key.	**Я не могу найти свой ключ.** [ja ne maˈgʊ najˈti svɔj klʲʊʧ]
Could you open my room, please?	**Откройте мой номер, пожалуйста.** [atkˈrɔjte mɔj ˈnɔmer, paˈʒaləstə]

Who's there?	**Кто там?** [ktɔ tam?]
Come in!	**Войдите!** [vajˈdite!]
Just a minute!	**Одну минуту!** [adˈnʊ miˈnʊtʊ!]
Not right now, please.	**Пожалуйста, не сейчас.** [paˈʒaləstə, ne seˈʧas]
Come to my room, please.	**Зайдите ко мне, пожалуйста.** [zajˈdite kamˈne, paˈʒaləstə]

I'd like to order food service.	**Я хочу сделать заказ еды в номер.** [ja haˈtʃu ˈsdelatʲ zaˈkas eˈdɪ v ˈnɔmer]
My room number is ...	**Мой номер комнаты ...** [mɔj ˈnɔmer ˈkɔmnatɪ ...]

I'm leaving ...	**Я уезжаю ...** [ja ueˈʒːaʲu ...]
We're leaving ...	**Мы уезжаем ...** [mɪ ueˈʒːaem ...]
right now	**сейчас** [seˈtʃas]
this afternoon	**сегодня после обеда** [seˈvɔdɲa ˈposle aˈbeda]
tonight	**сегодня вечером** [seˈvɔdɲa ˈwetʃerəm]
tomorrow	**завтра** [ˈzaftra]
tomorrow morning	**завтра утром** [ˈzaftra ˈutrəm]
tomorrow evening	**завтра вечером** [ˈzaftra ˈwetʃerəm]
the day after tomorrow	**послезавтра** [posleˈzaftra]

I'd like to pay.	**Я хотел бы /хотела бы/ рассчитаться.** [ja haˈtel /haˈtela/ bɪ rasɕiˈtatsa]
Everything was wonderful.	**Всё было отлично.** [vsʲo ˈbɪlə atˈlitʃnə]
Where can I get a taxi?	**Где я могу взять такси?** [gde ja maˈgʊ vzʲatʲ takˈsi?]
Would you call a taxi for me, please?	**Вызовите мне такси, пожалуйста.** [vɪzawite mne takˈsi, paˈʒaləstə]

Restaurant

Can I look at the menu, please?
Могу я посмотреть ваше меню?
[ma'gʊ ja pasmat'retʲ 'vaʃə me'nʲʉ?]

Table for one.
Столик для одного.
[stɔlik dʎa adna'vɔ]

There are two (three, four) of us.
Нас двое (трое, четверо).
[nas 'dvɔe ('trɔe, 'tʃetwərə)]

Smoking
Для курящих
[dʎa kʊ'rʲaɕih]

No smoking
Для некурящих
[dʎa nekʊ'rʲaɕih]

Excuse me! (addressing a waiter)
Будьте добры!
['bʊtʲte dab'rı!]

menu
меню
[me'nʲʉ]

wine list
карта вин
['karta win]

The menu, please.
Меню, пожалуйста.
[me'nʲʉ, pa'ʒaləstə]

Are you ready to order?
Вы готовы сделать заказ?
[vı ga'tɔvı 'sdelatʲ za'kas?]

What will you have?
Что вы будете заказывать?
[ʃtɔ vı 'bʊdete za'kazıvatʲ?]

I'll have …
Я буду …
[ja 'bʊdʊ …]

I'm a vegetarian.
Я вегетарианец /вегетарианка/.
[ja wegetari'anets /wegetari'anka/]

meat
мясо
['mʲasə]

fish
рыба
['rıba]

vegetables
овощи
['ɔvaɕi]

Do you have vegetarian dishes?
У вас есть вегетарианские блюда?
[u vas estʲ wegetari'anskie b'lʲʉda?]

I don't eat pork.
Я не ем свинину.
[ja ne 'em svi'ninʊ]

He /she/ doesn't eat meat.
Он /она/ не ест мясо.
[an /a'na/ ne est 'mʲasə]

I am allergic to …
У меня аллергия на …
[u me'ɲa aler'gija na …]

Would you please bring me ...	**Принесите мне, пожалуйста ...** [prine'site mne, pa'ʒaləstə ...]
salt | pepper | sugar	**соль | перец | сахар** [sɔlʲ | 'perets | 'sahar]
coffee | tea | dessert	**кофе | чай | десерт** ['kɔfe | ʧaj | de'sert]
water | sparkling | plain	**вода | с газом | без газа** [va'da | s 'gazəm | bes 'gaza]
a spoon | fork | knife	**ложка | вилка | нож** ['lɔʃka | 'wilka | nɔʃ]
a plate | napkin	**тарелка | салфетка** [ta'relka | sal'fetka]

Enjoy your meal!	**Приятного аппетита!** [pri'jatnəvə ape'tita!]
One more, please.	**Принесите ещё, пожалуйста.** [prine'site e'ɕʲo, pa'ʒaləstə]
It was very delicious.	**Было очень вкусно.** ['bɪlə 'ɔʧenʲ 'vkʊsnə]

---

check | change | tip	**счёт | сдача | чаевые** [ɕʲot | 'sdatʃə | ʧəi'vɪe]
Check, please. (Could I have the check, please?)	**Счёт, пожалуйста.** [ɕʲot, pa'ʒaləstə]
Can I pay by credit card?	**Могу я заплатить карточкой?** [ma'gʊ ja zapla'titʲ 'kartəʧkəj?]
I'm sorry, there's a mistake here.	**Извините, здесь ошибка.** [izwi'nite, zdesʲ a'ʃɪpka]

Shopping

Can I help you?
Могу я вам помочь?
[ma'gʊ ja vam pa'moʧ?]

Do you have ...?
У вас есть ...?
[u vas estʲ ...?]

I'm looking for ...
Я ищу ...
[ja i'ɕu ...]

I need ...
Мне нужен ...
[mne 'nʊʒən ...]

I'm just looking.
Я просто смотрю.
[ja 'prɔstə smat'rʲu]

We're just looking.
Мы просто смотрим.
[mɪ 'prɔstə 'smɔtrim]

I'll come back later.
Я зайду позже.
[ja zaj'dʊ 'pɔʒʒə]

We'll come back later.
Мы зайдём позже.
[mɪ zaj'dʲom 'pɔʒʒə]

discounts | sale
скидки | распродажа
['skitki | raspra'daʒa]

Would you please show me ...
Покажите мне, пожалуйста ...
[paka'ʒite mne, pa'ʒaləstə ...]

Would you please give me ...
Дайте мне, пожалуйста ...
[dajte mne, pa'ʒaləstə ...]

Can I try it on?
Могу я это примерить?
[ma'gʊ ja 'ɛtə pri'meritʲ?]

Excuse me, where's the fitting room?
Извините, где примерочная?
[izwi'nite, gde pri'merəʧnəja?]

Which color would you like?
Какой цвет вы хотите?
[ka'kɔj ʦwet vɪ ha'tite?]

size | length
размер | рост
[raz'mer | rɔst]

How does it fit?
Подошло?
[pada'ʃlɔ?]

How much is it?
Сколько это стоит?
['skɔlʲkə 'ɛtə 'stɔit?]

That's too expensive.
Это слишком дорого.
['ɛtə 'sliʃkəm 'dɔragə]

I'll take it.
Я возьму это.
[ja vɔzʲ'mʊ 'ɛtə]

Excuse me, where do I pay?
Извините, где касса?
[izwi'nite, gde 'kassa?]

Will you pay in cash or credit card?

Как вы будете платить?
[kak vɪ 'bʊdete pla'tit'?]

In cash | with credit card

наличными | карточкой
[na'litʃnɪmi | 'kartətʃkəj]

Do you want the receipt?

Вам нужен чек?
[vam 'nʊʒən tʃek?]

Yes, please.

Да, будьте добры.
[da, 'bʊt'te dab'rɪ]

No, it's OK.

Нет, не надо. Спасибо.
[net, ne 'nadə. spa'sibə]

Thank you. Have a nice day!

Спасибо. Всего хорошего!
[spa'sibə. vse'vɔ ha'roʃəvə!]

In town

Excuse me, please.
Извините, пожалуйста ...
[izwi'nite, pa'ʒaləstə …]

I'm looking for ...
Я ищу ...
[ja i'ɕu …]

the subway
метро
[me'trɔ]

my hotel
свою гостиницу
[svɔ'ʲʉ gas'tinitsu]

the movie theater
кинотеатр
[kinəte'atr]

a taxi stand
стоянку такси
[sta'janku tak'si]

an ATM
банкомат
[banka'mat]

a foreign exchange office
обмен валют
[ab'men va'lʲʉt]

an internet café
интернет-кафе
[intɛr'nɛt ka'fɛ]

... street
улицу ...
[ulitsu …]

this place
вот это место
[vɔt 'ɛtə 'mestə]

Do you know where ... is?
Вы не знаете, где находится ...?
[vɪ ne 'znaete, gde na'hoditsa …?]

Which street is this?
Как называется эта улица?
[kak nazɪ'vaetsa 'ɛta 'ulitsa?]

Show me where we are right now.
Покажите, где мы сейчас.
[paka'ʒite, gde mɪ se'tʃas]

Can I get there on foot?
Я дойду туда пешком?
[ja daj'du tʊ'da peʃ'kɔm?]

Do you have a map of the city?
У вас есть карта города?
[u vas estʲ 'karta 'gorada?]

How much is a ticket to get in?
Сколько стоит билет?
['skɔlʲkə 'stɔit bi'let?]

Can I take pictures here?
Здесь можно фотографировать?
[zdesʲ 'mɔʒnə fotagra'firəvatʲ?]

Are you open?
Вы открыты?
[vɪ atk'rɪtɪ?]

When do you open?

Во сколько вы открываетесь?
[vɔ 'skɔlʲkə vɪ atkrɪ'vaetesʲ?]

When do you close?

До которого часа вы работаете?
[dɔ ka'tɔrəvə 'ʧasa vɪ ra'bɔtaete?]

Money

money	**деньги** ['den^jgi]
cash	**наличные деньги** [na'litʃnɪe 'den^jgi]
paper money	**бумажные деньги** [bʊ'maʒnɪe 'den^jgi]
loose change	**мелочь** ['melɔtʃ]
check | change | tip	**счет | сдача | чаевые** [ɕʲot | 'sdatʃə | tʃəi'vɪe]
credit card	**кредитная карточка** [kre'ditnəja 'kartətʃka]
wallet	**бумажник** [bʊ'maʒnik]
to buy	**покупать** [pakʊ'pat^j]
to pay	**платить** [pla'tit^j]
fine	**штраф** [ʃtraf]
free	**бесплатно** [bisp'latnə]
Where can I buy ...?	**Где я могу купить ...?** [gde ja ma'gʊ kʊ'pit^j ...?]
Is the bank open now?	**Банк сейчас открыт?** [bank se'tʃas atk'rɪt?]
When does it open?	**Во сколько он открывается?** [vɔ 'skɔl^jkə ɔn atkrɪ'vaetsa?]
When does it close?	**До которого часа он работает?** [dɔ ka'tɔrəvə 'tʃasa an ra'bɔtaet?]
How much?	**Сколько?** ['skɔl^jkə?]
How much is this?	**Сколько это стоит?** ['skɔl^jkə 'ɛtə 'stɔit?]
That's too expensive.	**Это слишком дорого.** ['ɛtə 'sliʃkəm 'dɔragə]
Excuse me, where do I pay?	**Извините, где касса?** [izwi'nite, gde 'kassa?]
Check, please.	**Счёт, пожалуйста.** [ɕʲot, pa'ʒaləstə]

Can I pay by credit card?	**Могу я заплатить карточкой?** [ma'gʊ ja zapla'titʲ 'kartətʃkəj?]
Is there an ATM here?	**Здесь есть банкомат?** [zdesʲ estʲ banka'mat?]
I'm looking for an ATM.	**Мне нужен банкомат.** [mne 'nʊʒən banka'mat]

I'm looking for a foreign exchange office.	**Я ищу обмен валют.** [ja i'ɕu ab'men va'lʲʉt]
I'd like to change ...	**Я бы хотел /хотела/ поменять ...** [ja bɪ ha'tel /ha'tela/ pame'nʲatʲ ...]
What is the exchange rate?	**Какой курс обмена?** [ka'kɔj kʊrs ab'mena]
Do you need my passport?	**Вам нужен мой паспорт?** [vam 'nʊʒən mɔj 'paspərt?]

Time

What time is it?	**Который час?** [ka'tɔrij tʃas?]
When?	**Когда?** [kag'da?]
At what time?	**Во сколько?** [va 'skolʲkə?]
now | later | after …	**сейчас | позже | после …** [se'tʃas | 'pɔʐʐe | 'pɔsle …]

one o'clock	**Час дня** [tʃas dɲa]
one fifteen	**Час пятнадцать** [tʃas pit'natsatʲ]
one thirty	**Час тридцать** [tʃas tʲritʦatʲ]
one forty-five	**Без пятнадцати два** [bez pit'natsati dva]

one | two | three	**один | два | три** [a'din | dva | tri]
four | five | six	**четыре | пять | шесть** [tʃe'tɨre | pʲatʲ | ʃɛstʲ]
seven | eight | nine	**семь | восемь | девять** [semʲ | 'vɔsemʲ | 'devʲatʲ]
ten | eleven | twelve	**десять | одиннадцать | двенадцать** ['desʲatʲ | a'dinnatsatʲ | dwi'natsatʲ]

in …	**через …** [tʃerez …]
five minutes	**5 минут** [pʲatʲ mi'nut]
ten minutes	**10 минут** ['desʲatʲ mi'nut]
fifteen minutes	**15 минут** [pit'natsatʲ mi'nut]
twenty minutes	**20 минут** ['dvatsatʲ mi'nut]

half an hour	**полчаса** [pɔltʃa'sa]
an hour	**один час** [a'din tʃas]

in the morning	**утром** ['utrəm]
early in the morning	**рано утром** [ranə 'utrəm]
this morning	**сегодня утром** [se'vɔdɲa 'utrəm]
tomorrow morning	**завтра утром** ['zaftrə 'utrəm]
at noon	**в обед** [v a'bet]
in the afternoon	**после обеда** ['posle a'beda]
in the evening	**вечером** ['wetʃerəm]
tonight	**сегодня вечером** [se'vɔdɲa 'wetʃerəm]
at night	**ночью** ['nɔtʃʉ]
yesterday	**вчера** [vtʃe'ra]
today	**сегодня** [si'vɔdɲa]
tomorrow	**завтра** ['zaftra]
the day after tomorrow	**послезавтра** [posle'zaftra]
What day is it today?	**Какой сегодня день?** [ka'kɔj si'vɔdɲa denʲ?]
It's ...	**Сегодня ...** [se'vɔdɲa ...]
Monday	**понедельник** [pani'delʲnik]
Tuesday	**вторник** ['ftornik]
Wednesday	**среда** [sri'da]
Thursday	**четверг** [tʃet'werk]
Friday	**пятница** ['pʲatnitsa]
Saturday	**суббота** [sʊ'bota]
Sunday	**воскресение** [vaskrə'seɲje]

Greetings. Introductions

Hello.

Здравствуйте.
['zdrastvujte]

Pleased to meet you.

Рад /рада/ с вами познакомиться.
[rad /'rada/ s 'vami pazna'komitsa]

Me too.

Я тоже.
[ja 'toʒɛ]

I'd like you to meet ...

Знакомьтесь. Это ...
[zna'komʲtesʲ. 'ɛtə ...]

Nice to meet you.

Очень приятно.
[ɔʧenʲ pri'jatnə]

How are you?

Как вы? | Как у вас дела?
[kak vɪ? | kak u vas de'la?]

My name is ...

Меня зовут ...
[mi'ɲa za'vʊt ...]

His name is ...

Его зовут ...
[e'vɔ za'vʊt ...]

Her name is ...

Её зовут ...
[eʲo za'vʊt ...]

What's your name?

Как вас зовут?
[kak vas za'vʊt?]

What's his name?

Как его зовут?
[kak e'vɔ za'vʊt?]

What's her name?

Как ее зовут?
[kak eʲo za'vʊt?]

What's your last name?

Как ваша фамилия?
[kak 'vaʃʌ fa'milija?]

You can call me ...

Зовите меня ...
[za'wite meʲɲa ...]

Where are you from?

Откуда вы?
[at'kʊda vɪ]

I'm from ...

Я из ...
[ja iz ...]

What do you do for a living?

Кем вы работаете?
[kem vɪ ra'botaete?]

Who is this?

Кто это?
[ktɔ 'ɛtə?]

Who is he?

Кто он?
[ktɔ ɔn?]

Who is she?

Кто она?
[ktɔ a'na?]

Who are they?

Кто они?
[ktɔ a'ni?]

This is ...	**Это ...** ['ɛtə ...]
my friend (masc.)	**мой друг** [mɔj drʊk]
my friend (fem.)	**моя подруга** [ma'ja pad'rʊga]
my husband	**мой муж** [mɔj mʊʃ]
my wife	**моя жена** [ma'ja ʒi'na]

my father	**мой отец** [mɔj a'teʦ]
my mother	**моя мама** [ma'ja 'mama]
my brother	**мой брат** [mɔj brat]
my sister	**моя сестра** [ma'ja sist'ra]
my son	**мой сын** [mɔj sɪn]
my daughter	**моя дочь** [ma'ja dɔʧ]

This is our son.	**Это наш сын.** ['ɛtə naʃ sɪn]
This is our daughter.	**Это наша дочь.** ['ɛtə 'naʃʌ dɔʧ]
These are my children.	**Это мои дети.** ['ɛtə ma'i 'deti]
These are our children.	**Это наши дети.** ['ɛtə 'naʃi 'deti]

Farewells

Good bye!	**До свидания!** [dɔ swi'danija!]
Bye! (inform.)	**Пока!** [pa'ka!]
See you tomorrow.	**До завтра.** [dɔ 'zaftra]
See you soon.	**До встречи.** [dɔ vstrʲetʃi]
See you at seven.	**Встретимся в семь.** [vstrʲetimsʲa v semʲ]
Have fun!	**Развлекайтесь!** [razvle'kajtesʲ!]
Talk to you later.	**Поговорим попозже.** [pagava'rim pa'pɔʒʒə]
Have a nice weekend.	**Удачных выходных.** [u'datʃnɨh vɨhad'nɨh]
Good night.	**Спокойной ночи.** [spa'kɔjnəj 'nɔtʃi]
It's time for me to go.	**Мне пора.** [mne pa'ra]
I have to go.	**Мне надо идти.** [mne 'nadə it'ti]
I will be right back.	**Я сейчас вернусь.** [ja se'tʃas wer'nusʲ]
It's late.	**Уже поздно.** [u'ʒɛ 'pɔzdnə]
I have to get up early.	**Мне рано вставать.** [mne 'ranə vsta'vatʲ]
I'm leaving tomorrow.	**Я завтра уезжаю.** [ja 'zaftra ue'ʐʐaʲʉ]
We're leaving tomorrow.	**Мы завтра уезжаем.** [mɨ 'zaftra ue'ʐʐaem]
Have a nice trip!	**Счастливой поездки!** [ɕas'livəj pa'eztki!]
It was nice meeting you.	**Было приятно с вами познакомиться.** ['bɨlə pri'jatnə s 'vami pazna'kɔmitsa]
It was nice talking to you.	**Было приятно с вами пообщаться.** ['bɨlə pri'jatnə s 'vami paab'ɕatsa]

Thanks for everything.	**Спасибо за всё.** [spa'sibə za 'vsʲo]
I had a very good time.	**Я прекрасно провёл /провела/ время.** [ja preˈkrasnə praˈwʲol /praweˈla/ 'vremʲa]
We had a very good time.	**Мы прекрасно провели время.** [mɪ preˈkrasnə praweˈli 'vremʲa]
It was really great.	**Всё было замечательно.** [vsʲo 'bɪlə zameˈtʃatelʲnə]
I'm going to miss you.	**Я буду скучать.** [ja 'bʊdʊ skʊˈtʃatʲ]
We're going to miss you.	**Мы будем скучать.** [mɪ 'bʊdem skʊˈtʃatʲ]
Good luck!	**Удачи! Счастливо!** [uˈdatʃi! 'ɕaslivə!]
Say hi to ...	**Передавайте привет …** [peredaˈvajte priˈwet …]

Foreign language

I don't understand.	**Я не понимаю.**
	[ja ne pani'maᵼ]
Write it down, please.	**Напишите это, пожалуйста.**
	[napi'ʃite 'ɛtə, pa'ʒaləstə]
Do you speak ...?	**Вы знаете ...?**
	[vɪ 'znaete ...?]

I speak a little bit of ...	**Я немного знаю ...**
	[ja nem'nɔgə 'znaᵼ ...]
English	**английский**
	[ang'lijskij]
Turkish	**турецкий**
	[tʊ'retskij]
Arabic	**арабский**
	[a'rapskij]
French	**французский**
	[fran'tsuskij]

German	**немецкий**
	[ne'metskij]
Italian	**итальянский**
	[ita'ljanskij]
Spanish	**испанский**
	[is'panskij]
Portuguese	**португальский**
	[partʊgal'skij]
Chinese	**китайский**
	[ki'tajskij]
Japanese	**японский**
	[ja'ponskij]

Can you repeat that, please.	**Повторите, пожалуйста.**
	[pavta'rite, pa'ʒaləstə]
I understand.	**Я понимаю.**
	[ja pani'maᵼ]
I don't understand.	**Я не понимаю.**
	[ja ne pani'maᵼ]
Please speak more slowly.	**Говорите медленнее, пожалуйста.**
	[gava'rite 'medlenee, pa'ʒaləstə]

Is that correct? (Am I saying it right?)	**Это правильно?**
	['ɛtə 'prawil'nə?]
What is this? (What does this mean?)	**Что это?**
	[ʃto 'ɛtə?]

Apologies

Excuse me, please.	**Извините, пожалуйста.** [izwi'nite, pa'ʒaləstə]
I'm sorry.	**Я сожалею.** [ja saʒə'leʉ]
I'm really sorry.	**Мне очень жаль.** [mne 'ɔtʃenʲ ʒalʲ]
Sorry, it's my fault.	**Виноват /Виновата/, это моя вина.** [wina'vat /wina'vata/, 'ɛtə ma'ja wi'na]
My mistake.	**Моя ошибка.** [ma'ja a'ʃipka]
May I ...?	**Могу я ...?** [ma'gʊ ja ...?]
Do you mind if I ...?	**Вы не будете возражать, если я ...?** [vɪ ne 'bʊdete vazra'ʒatʲ, 'esli ja ...?]
It's OK.	**Ничего страшного.** [nitʃe'vɔ 'straʃnəvə]
It's all right.	**Всё в порядке.** [vsʲo v pa'rʲatke]
Don't worry about it.	**Не беспокойтесь.** [ne bespa'kɔjtesʲ]

Agreement

Yes.
Да.
[da]

Yes, sure.
Да, конечно.
[da, ka'neʃnə]

OK (Good!)
Хорошо!
[hara'ʃo!]

Very well.
Очень хорошо.
['otʃenʲ hara'ʃo]

Certainly!
Конечно!
[ka'neʃnə!]

I agree.
Я согласен /согласна/.
[ja sag'lasen /sag'lasna/]

That's correct.
Верно.
['wernə]

That's right.
Правильно.
['prawilʲnə]

You're right.
Вы правы.
[vɪ 'pravɪ]

I don't mind.
Я не возражаю.
[ja ne vazra'ʒaʲʉ]

Absolutely right.
Совершенно верно.
[sawer'ʃɛnnə 'wernə]

It's possible.
Это возможно.
['ɛtə vaz'moʒnə]

That's a good idea.
Это хорошая мысль.
[ɛtə ha'roʃeja mɪslʲ]

I can't say no.
Не могу отказать.
[ne ma'gʊ atka'zatʲ]

I'd be happy to.
Буду рад /рада/.
[bʊdʊ rad /'rada/]

With pleasure.
С удовольствием.
[s uda'volʲstwiem]

Refusal. Expressing doubt

No.	**Нет.** [net]
Certainly not.	**Конечно нет.** [ka'neʃnə net]

I don't agree.	**Я не согласен /не согласна/.** [ja ne sag'lasen /ne sag'lasna/]
I don't think so.	**Я так не думаю.** [ja tak ne 'dʊmaʲʉ]
It's not true.	**Это неправда.** ['ɛtə nep'ravda]

You are wrong.	**Вы неправы.** [vɪ nep'ravɪ]
I think you are wrong.	**Я думаю, что вы неправы.** [ja 'dʊmaʲʉ, ʃtɔ vɪ nep'ravɪ]

I'm not sure.	**Не уверен /не уверена/.** [ne u'veren /ne u'verena/]
It's impossible.	**Это невозможно.** ['ɛtə nevaz'mɔʒnə]
Nothing of the kind (sort)!	**Ничего подобного!** [nitʃe'vɔ pa'dɔbnəvə!]

The exact opposite.	**Наоборот!** [naaba'rɔt!]
I'm against it.	**Я против.** [ja 'prɔtiv]
I don't care.	**Мне всё равно.** [mne vsʲo rav'nɔ]
I have no idea.	**Понятия не имею.** [pa'ɲatija ne i'meʲʉ]
I doubt that.	**Сомневаюсь, что это так.** [samne'vaʲʉsʲ, ʃtɔ 'ɛtə tak]

Sorry, I can't.	**Извините, я не могу.** [izwi'nite, ja ne ma'gʊ]
Sorry, I don't want to.	**Извините, я не хочу.** [izwi'nite, ja ne ha'tʃu]

Thank you, but I don't need this.	**Спасибо, мне это не нужно.** [spa'sibə, mne 'ɛtə ne 'nʊʒnə]
It's late.	**Уже поздно.** [u'ʒɛ 'pɔzdnə]

I have to get up early.

Мне рано вставать.
[mne 'ranə vsta'vatʲ]

I don't feel well.

Я плохо себя чувствую.
[ja 'plɔhə se'bʲa 'tʃustvʊʲʉ]

Expressing gratitude

Thank you.	**Спасибо.** [spa'sibə]
Thank you very much.	**Спасибо большое.** [spa'sibə balʲ'ʃoe]
I really appreciate it.	**Очень признателен /признательна/.** [ɔʧenʲ priz'natelen /priz'natelʲna/]
I'm really grateful to you.	**Я вам благодарен /благодарна/.** [ja vam blaga'daren /blaga'darna/]
We are really grateful to you.	**Мы Вам благодарны.** [mɪ vam blaga'darnɪ]
Thank you for your time.	**Спасибо, что потратили время.** [spa'sibə, ʃtɔ pat'ratili 'vremʲa]
Thanks for everything.	**Спасибо за всё.** [spa'sibə za 'vsʲo]
Thank you for ...	**Спасибо за ...** [spa'sibə za ...]
your help	**вашу помощь** [vaʃʊ 'pɔmaɕ]
a nice time	**хорошее время** [ha'rɔʃee 'vremʲa]
a wonderful meal	**прекрасную еду** [pre'krasnʊʲʉ e'dʊ]
a pleasant evening	**приятный вечер** [pri'jatnɪj 'weʧer]
a wonderful day	**замечательный день** [zami'ʧatelʲnɪj denʲ]
an amazing journey	**интересную экскурсию** [inte'resnʊʲʉ ɛks'kʊrsiʲʉ]
Don't mention it.	**Не за что.** [ne za ʃtə]
You are welcome.	**Не стоит благодарности.** [ne 'stɔit blaga'darnasti]
Any time.	**Всегда пожалуйста.** [vseg'da pa'ʒaləsta]
My pleasure.	**Был рад /Была рада/ помочь.** [bɪl rad /bɪ'la 'rada/ pa'mɔʧ]
Forget it. It's alright.	**Забудьте. Всё в порядке.** [za'butʲte. fsʲo f pɔ'rʲatke]
Don't worry about it.	**Не беспокойтесь.** [ne bespa'kɔjtesʲ]

Congratulations. Best wishes

Congratulations!	**Поздравляю!** [pazdrav'ʎaʲʉ!]
Happy birthday!	**С днём рождения!** [s 'dnʲom raʒ'denija!]
Merry Christmas!	**Весёлого рождества!** [weˈsʲolevə raʒdestˈva!]
Happy New Year!	**С Новым годом!** [s 'nɔvɪm 'gɔdəm!]
Happy Easter!	**Со Светлой Пасхой!** [sɔ 'swetləj 'pashəj!]
Happy Hanukkah!	**Счастливой Хануки!** [ɕas'livej 'hanʊki!]
I'd like to propose a toast.	**У меня есть тост.** [u me'ɲa estʲ tɔst]
Cheers!	**За ваше здоровье!** [za 'vaʃə zda'rɔvje]
Let's drink to ...!	**Выпьем за ... !** ['vɪpjem za ... !]
To our success!	**За наш успех!** [za naʃ us'peh!]
To your success!	**За ваш успех!** [za vaʃ us'peh!]
Good luck!	**Удачи!** [u'datʃi!]
Have a nice day!	**Приятного вам дня!** [pri'jatnəvə vam dɲa!]
Have a good holiday!	**Хорошего вам отдыха!** [ha'rɔʃəvə vam 'ɔtdɪha!]
Have a safe journey!	**Удачной поездки!** [u'datʃnəj pa'eztki!]
I hope you get better soon!	**Желаю вам скорого выздоровления!** [ʒe'laʲʉ vam 'skɔrəvə vɪzdarav'lenija!]

Socializing

Why are you sad?	**Почему вы расстроены?** [patʃe'mʊ vɪ rast'rɔenɪ?]
Smile! Cheer up!	**Улыбнитесь!** [ulɪb'nitesʲ!]
Are you free tonight?	**Вы не заняты сегодня вечером?** [vɪ ne zaɲatɪ se'vɔdɲa 'wetʃerəm?]
May I offer you a drink?	**Могу я предложить вам выпить?** [ma'gʊ ja predla'ʒitʲ vam 'vɪpitʲ?]
Would you like to dance?	**Не хотите потанцевать?** [ne ha'tite patantse'vatʲ?]
Let's go to the movies.	**Может сходим в кино?** ['mɔʒet 'shɔdim v ki'nɔ?]
May I invite you to ...?	**Могу я пригласить вас в ...?** [ma'gʊ ja prigla'sitʲ vas v ...?]
a restaurant	**ресторан** [resta'ran]
the movies	**кино** [ki'nɔ]
the theater	**театр** [te'atr]
go for a walk	**на прогулку** [na pra'gʊlkʊ]
At what time?	**Во сколько?** [va 'skɔlʲkə?]
tonight	**сегодня вечером** [se'vɔdɲa 'wetʃerəm]
at six	**в 6 часов** [v ʃestʲ tʃa'sɔf]
at seven	**в 7 часов** [v semʲ tʃa'sɔf]
at eight	**в 8 часов** [v 'vɔsemʲ tʃa'sɔf]
at nine	**в 9 часов** [v 'devʲatʲ tʃa'sɔf]
Do you like it here?	**Вам здесь нравится?** [vam zdesʲ 'nrawitsa?]
Are you here with someone?	**Вы здесь с кем-то?** [vɪ zdesʲ s 'kem tə?]
I'm with my friend.	**Я с другом /подругой/.** [ja s 'drʊgəm /pad'rʊgəj/]

I'm with my friends.	**Я с друзьями.** [ja s drʊ'zjʲami]
No, I'm alone.	**Я один /одна/.** [ja a'din /ad'na/]

Do you have a boyfriend?	**У тебя есть приятель?** [u te'bʲa estʲ pri'jatelʲ?]
I have a boyfriend.	**У меня есть друг.** [u me'ɲa estʲ drʊk]
Do you have a girlfriend?	**У тебя есть подружка?** [u te'bʲa estʲ pad'rʊʃka?]
I have a girlfriend.	**У меня есть девушка.** [u me'ɲa estʲ 'devʊʃka]

Can I see you again?	**Мы еще встретимся?** [mɪ e'ɕʲo vst'retimsʲa?]
Can I call you?	**Можно я тебе позвоню?** [mɔʒnə ja te'be pazva'nʲʉ?]
Call me. (Give me a call.)	**Позвони мне.** [pazva'ni mne]
What's your number?	**Какой у тебя номер?** [ka'kɔj u te'bʲa 'nɔmer?]
I miss you.	**Я скучаю по тебе.** [ja skʊ'tʃaʲʉ pa te'be]

You have a beautiful name.	**У вас очень красивое имя.** [u vas 'ɔtʃenʲ kra'sivae 'imʲa]
I love you.	**Я тебя люблю.** [ja te'bʲa lʲʉb'lʲʉ]
Will you marry me?	**Выходи за меня.** [vɪha'di za me'ɲa]
You're kidding!	**Вы шутите!** [vɪ 'ʃʊtite!]
I'm just kidding.	**Я просто шучу.** [ja 'prɔstə ʃʊ'tʃu]

Are you serious?	**Вы серьезно?** [vɪ se'rjɔznə?]
I'm serious.	**Я серьёзно.** [ja se'rjʲɔznə]
Really?!	**Правда?!** ['pravda?!]
It's unbelievable!	**Это невероятно!** ['ɛtə newera'jatnə]
I don't believe you.	**Я вам не верю.** [ja vam ne 'werʲʉ]
I can't.	**Я не могу.** [ja ne ma'gʊ]
I don't know.	**Я не знаю.** [ja ne 'znaʲʉ]
I don't understand you.	**Я вас не понимаю.** [ja vas ne pani'maʲʉ]

Please go away.

Уйдите, пожалуйста.
[uj'dite, pa'ʒaləstə]

Leave me alone!

Оставьте меня в покое!
[as'tavᶥte meʲɲa v pa'kɔe!]

I can't stand him.

Я его не выношу.
[ja e'gɔ ne vɪna'ʃʊ]

You are disgusting!

Вы отвратительны!
[vɪ atvra'titelᶥnɪ!]

I'll call the police!

Я вызову полицию!
[ja 'vɪzavʊ pa'litsiᶥʉ!]

Sharing impressions. Emotions

I like it.	**Мне это нравится.** [mne 'ɛtə 'nrawitsa]
Very nice.	**Очень мило.** ['ɔtʃenʲ 'milə]
That's great!	**Это здорово!** ['ɛtə 'zdɔrɔvɛ!]
It's not bad.	**Это неплохо.** ['ɛtə nep'lɔhə]

I don't like it.	**Мне это не нравится.** [mne 'ɛtə ne 'nrawitsa]
It's not good.	**Это нехорошо.** ['ɛtə nehara'ʃɔ]
It's bad.	**Это плохо.** ['ɛtə 'plɔhə]
It's very bad.	**Это очень плохо.** ['ɛtə 'ɔtʃenʲ 'plɔhə]
It's disgusting.	**Это отвратительно.** ['ɛtə atvra'titelʲnə]

I'm happy.	**Я счастлив /счастлива/.** [ja 'ɕːasliv /'ɕːasliva/]
I'm content.	**Я доволен /довольна/.** [ja da'vɔlen /da'vɔlʲna/]
I'm in love.	**Я влюблён /влюблена/.** [ja vlʲʉb'lʲon /vlʲʉble'na/]
I'm calm.	**Я спокоен /спокойна/.** [ja spa'kɔen /spa'kɔjna/]
I'm bored.	**Мне скучно.** [mne 'skuʃnə]

I'm tired.	**Я устал /устала/.** [ja us'tal /us'tala/]
I'm sad.	**Мне грустно.** [mne 'grusnə]
I'm frightened.	**Я напуган /напугана/.** [ja na'pugan /na'pugana/]

I'm angry.	**Я злюсь.** [ja zlʲʉsʲ]
I'm worried.	**Я волнуюсь.** [ja val'nuʲʉsʲ]
I'm nervous.	**Я нервничаю.** [ja 'nervnitʃaʲʉ]

I'm jealous. (envious) **Я завидую.**
[ja za'widʊʲʉ]

I'm surprised. **Я удивлён /удивлена/.**
[ja udiv'lʲon /udivle'na/]

I'm perplexed. **Я озадачен /озадачена/.**
[ja aza'datʃen /aza'datʃena/]

Problems. Accidents

I've got a problem.	**У меня проблема.** [u me'ɲa prab'lema]
We've got a problem.	**У нас проблема.** [u nas prab'lema]
I'm lost.	**Я заблудился /заблудилась/.** [ja zablu'dilsʲa /zablu'dilasʲ/]
I missed the last bus (train).	**Я опоздал на последний автобус (поезд).** [ja apaz'dal na pas'lednij aft'ɔbus ('pɔest)]
I don't have any money left.	**У меня совсем не осталось денег.** [u me'ɲa sav'sem ne as'taləsʲ 'denek]

I've lost my …	**Я потерял /потеряла/ …** [ja pate'rʲal /pate'rʲala/ …]
Someone stole my …	**У меня украли …** [u me'ɲa uk'rali …]
passport	**паспорт** ['paspərt]
wallet	**бумажник** [bu'maʒnik]
papers	**документы** [daku'mentɪ]
ticket	**билет** [bi'let]

money	**деньги** ['denʲgi]
handbag	**сумку** ['sumku]
camera	**фотоаппарат** ['fota apa'rat]
laptop	**ноутбук** [nɔut'buk]
tablet computer	**планшет** [plan'ʃət]
mobile phone	**телефон** [tele'fɔn]

Help me!	**Помогите!** [pama'gite]
What's happened?	**Что случилось?** [ʃtɔ slu'tʃiləsʲ?]

fire	пожар
	[pa'ʒar]
shooting	стрельба
	[strel^jba]
murder	убийство
	[u'bijstvə]
explosion	взрыв
	[vzrɪv]
fight	драка
	['draka]

Call the police!	Вызовите полицию!
	['vɪzawite pa'litsɨ^jʉ!]
Please hurry up!	Пожалуйста, быстрее!
	[pa'ʒaləstə, bɪst'ree!]
I'm looking for the police station.	Я ищу полицейский участок.
	[ja i'ɕu pali'tsɛjskij u'tʃastək]
I need to make a call.	Мне нужно позвонить.
	[mne 'nuʒnə pazva'nit^j]
May I use your phone?	Могу я позвонить?
	[ma'gʊ ja pazva'nit^j?]

I've been …	Меня …
	[mi'ɲa …]
mugged	ограбили
	[ag'rabili]
robbed	обокрали
	[abak'rali]
raped	изнасиловали
	[izna'siləvali]
attacked (beaten up)	избили
	[iz'bili]

Are you all right?	С вами все в порядке?
	[s 'vami vs^jo v pa'r^jatke?]
Did you see who it was?	Вы видели, кто это был?
	[vɪ 'wideli, kto 'ɛtə bɪl?]
Would you be able to recognize the person?	Вы сможете его узнать?
	[vɪ s'moʒete e'vɔ uz'nat^j?]
Are you sure?	Вы точно уверены?
	[vɪ 'totʃnə u'werenɪ?]

Please calm down.	Пожалуйста, успокойтесь.
	[pa'ʒaləstə, uspa'kojtes^j]
Take it easy!	Спокойнее!
	[spa'kojnee!]
Don't worry!	Не беспокойтесь.
	[ne bespa'kojtes^j]
Everything will be fine.	Всё будет хорошо.
	[vs^jo 'bʊdet hara'ʃɔ]
Everything's all right.	Всё в порядке.
	[vs^jo v pa'r^jatke]

Come here, please.

Подойдите, пожалуйста.
[padaj'dite, pa'ʒaləstə]

I have some questions for you.

У меня к вам несколько вопросов.
[u me'ɲa k vam 'neskalʲkə vap'rɔsəf]

Wait a moment, please.

Подождите, пожалуйста.
[padaʒ'dite, pa'ʒaləstə]

Do you have any I.D.?

У вас есть документы?
[u vas estʲ daku'mentɪ?]

Thanks. You can leave now.

Спасибо. Вы можете идти.
[spa'sibə. vɪ 'mɔʒɛte it'ti]

Hands behind your head!

Руки за голову!
['rʊki 'zagalavʊ!]

You're under arrest!

Вы арестованы!
[vɪ ares'tɔvanɪ!]

Health problems

Please help me.	**Помогите, пожалуйста.** [pama'gite, pa'ʒaləstə]
I don't feel well.	**Мне плохо.** [mne 'pləhə]
My husband doesn't feel well.	**Моему мужу плохо.** [mae'mʊ 'mʊʒu 'pləhə]
My son …	**Моему сыну …** [mae'mʊ 'sınʊ …]
My father …	**Моему отцу …** [mae'mʊ at'ʦu …]
My wife doesn't feel well.	**Моей жене плохо.** [ma'ej ʒɛne 'pləhə]
My daughter …	**Моей дочери …** [ma'ej 'dɔʧeri …]
My mother …	**Моей матери …** [ma'ej 'materi …]
I've got a …	**У меня болит …** [u me'ɲa ba'lit …]
headache	**голова** [gala'va]
sore throat	**горло** ['gɔrlə]
stomach ache	**живот** [ʒı'vɔt]
toothache	**зуб** [zup]
I feel dizzy.	**У меня кружится голова.** [u me'ɲa krʊʒitsa gala'va]
He has a fever.	**У него температура.** [u ne'vɔ tempera'tʊra]
She has a fever.	**У неё температура.** [u ne'o tempera'tʊra]
I can't breathe.	**Я не могу дышать.** [ja ne ma'gʊ dı'ʃʌtʲ]
I'm short of breath.	**Я задыхаюсь.** [ja zadı'haʲʊsʲ]
I am asthmatic.	**Я астматик.** [ja ast'matik]
I am diabetic.	**Я диабетик.** [ja dia'betik]

I can't sleep.	**У меня бессонница.** [u me'ɲa bes'sɔnitsa]
food poisoning	**пищевое отравление** [piɕe'vɔe atrav'lenie]

It hurts here.	**Болит вот здесь.** [ba'lit vɔt zdesʲ]
Help me!	**Помогите!** [pama'gite!]
I am here!	**Я здесь!** [ja zdesʲ!]
We are here!	**Мы здесь!** [mɪ zdesʲ!]
Get me out of here!	**Вытащите меня!** ['vɪtaɕite me'ɲa!]
I need a doctor.	**Мне нужен врач.** [mne 'nʊʒən vratʃ]
I can't move.	**Я не могу двигаться.** [ja ne ma'gʊ 'dvigatsa]
I can't move my legs.	**Я не чувствую ног.** [ja ne 'tʃustvʊʉ nɔk]

I have a wound.	**Я ранен /ранена/.** [ja 'ranen /'ranena/]
Is it serious?	**Это серьезно?** ['ɛtə se'rʲʲoznə?]
My documents are in my pocket.	**Мои документы в кармане.** [ma'i dakʊ'mentɪ v kar'mane]
Calm down!	**Успокойтесь!** [uspa'kɔjtesʲ!]
May I use your phone?	**Могу я позвонить?** [ma'gʊ ja pazva'nitʲ?]

Call an ambulance!	**Вызовите скорую!** [vɪzawite 'skɔrʊʉ!]
It's urgent!	**Это срочно!** ['ɛtə 'srɔtʃnə!]
It's an emergency!	**Это очень срочно!** ['ɛtə 'ɔtʃenʲ 'srɔtʃnə!]
Please hurry up!	**Пожалуйста, быстрее!** [pa'ʒaləstə, bɪst'ree!]
Would you please call a doctor?	**Вызовите врача, пожалуйста.** [vɪzawite vra'tʃa, pa'ʒaləstə]
Where is the hospital?	**Скажите, где больница?** [ska'ʒite, gde balʲ'nitsa?]

How are you feeling?	**Как вы себя чувствуете?** [kak vɪ se'bʲa 'tʃustvʊete?]
Are you all right?	**С вами все в порядке?** [s 'vami vsʲɔ v pa'rʲatke?]
What's happened?	**Что случилось?** [ʃto slu'tʃiləsʲ?]

I feel better now.

Мне уже лучше.
[mne u'ʒe 'lutʃɛ]

It's OK.

Всё в порядке.
[vsʲo v pa'rʲatke]

It's all right.

Всё хорошо.
[vsʲo hara'ʃo]

At the pharmacy

pharmacy (drugstore)	**Аптека** [ap'teka]
24-hour pharmacy	**круглосуточная аптека** [krʊgla'sʊtətʃnəja ap'teka]
Where is the closest pharmacy?	**Где ближайшая аптека?** [gde bli'ʒajʃəja ap'teka?]
Is it open now?	**Она сейчас открыта?** [a'na se'tʃas atk'rɪta?]
At what time does it open?	**Во сколько она открывается?** [va 'skolʲkə a'na atkrɪ'vaetsa?]
At what time does it close?	**До которого часа она работает?** [dɔ ka'tɔrəvə 'tʃasa a'na ra'bɔtaet?]
Is it far?	**Это далеко?** ['ɛtə dale'kɔ?]
Can I get there on foot?	**Я дойду туда пешком?** [ja daj'dʊ tʊ'da peʃ'kɔm?]
Can you show me on the map?	**Покажите мне на карте, пожалуйста.** [paka'ʒite mne na 'karte, pa'ʒaləstə]
Please give me something for ...	**Дайте мне, что-нибудь от ...** ['dajte mne, ʃto ni'bʊtʲ ɔt …]
a headache	**головной боли** [galav'nɔj 'bɔli]
a cough	**кашля** ['kaʃʎa]
a cold	**простуды** [pras'tʊdɪ]
the flu	**гриппа** ['gripa]
a fever	**температуры** [tempera'tʊrɪ]
a stomach ache	**боли в желудке** ['bɔli v ʒɪ'lutke]
nausea	**тошноты** [taʃna'tɪ]
diarrhea	**диареи** [dia'rei]
constipation	**запора** [za'pɔra]
pain in the back	**боль в спине** [bɔlʲ v spi'ne]

chest pain	**боль в груди** ['bolʲ v grʊ'di]
side stitch	**боль в боку** [bolʲ v ba'kʊ]
abdominal pain	**боль в животе** ['bolʲ v ʒiva'te]

pill	**таблетка** [tab'letka]
ointment, cream	**мазь, крем** [mazʲ, krem]
syrup	**сироп** [si'rɔp]
spray	**спрей** [sprɛj]
drops	**капли** ['kapli]

You need to go to the hospital.	**Вам нужно в больницу.** [vam 'nʊʒnə v balʲ'nitsu]
health insurance	**страховка** [stra'hovka]
prescription	**рецепт** [re'tsept]
insect repellant	**средство от насекомых** ['sredstvə at nase'komıh]
Band Aid	**лейкопластырь** [lejkə'plastırʲ]

The bare minimum

Excuse me, ...	**Извините, ...** [izwi'nite, ...]
Hello.	**Здравствуйте.** ['zdrastvʊjte]
Thank you.	**Спасибо.** [spa'sibə]
Good bye.	**До свидания.** [da swi'danija]
Yes.	**Да.** [da]
No.	**Нет.** [net]
I don't know.	**Я не знаю.** [ja ne 'znaʲʉ]
Where?	Where to?	When?	**Где?	Куда?	Когда?** [gde?	kʊ'da?	kag'da?]

I need ...	**Мне нужен ...** [mne 'nʊʒən ...]
I want ...	**Я хочу ...** [ja ha'ʧu ...]
Do you have ...?	**У вас есть ...?** [u vas estʲ ...?]
Is there a ... here?	**Здесь есть ...?** [zdesʲ estʲ ...?]
May I ...?	**Я могу ...?** [ja ma'gʊ ...?]
..., please (polite request)	**пожалуйста** [pa'ʒaləstə]

I'm looking for ...	**Я ищу ...** [ja i'ɕu ...]
restroom	**туалет** [tʊa'let]
ATM	**банкомат** [banka'mat]
pharmacy (drugstore)	**аптеку** [ap'tekʊ]
hospital	**больницу** [balʲ'niʦu]
police station	**полицейский участок** [pali'ʦɛjskij u'ʧastək]
subway	**метро** [met'rɔ]

taxi	**такси** [tak'si]
train station	**вокзал** [vak'zal]

My name is ...	**Меня зовут ...** [mi'ɲa za'vʊt ...]
What's your name?	**Как вас зовут?** [kak vas za'vʊt?]
Could you please help me?	**Помогите мне, пожалуйста.** [pama'gite mne, pa'ʒaləstə]
I've got a problem.	**У меня проблема.** [u me'ɲa prab'lema]
I don't feel well.	**Мне плохо.** [mne 'plɔhə]
Call an ambulance!	**Вызовите скорую!** [vɪzawite 'skɔrʊʲʉ!]
May I make a call?	**Могу я позвонить?** [ma'gʊ ja pazva'nitʲ?]

I'm sorry.	**Извините.** [izwi'nite]
You're welcome.	**Пожалуйста.** [pa'ʒaləstə]

I, me	**я** [ja]
you (inform.)	**ты** [tɪ]
he	**он** [ɔn]
she	**она** [a'na]
they (masc.)	**они** [a'ni]
they (fem.)	**они** [a'ni]
we	**мы** [mɪ]
you (pl)	**вы** [vɪ]
you (sg, form.)	**Вы** [vɪ]

ENTRANCE	**ВХОД** [vhɔt]
EXIT	**ВЫХОД** ['vɪhət]
OUT OF ORDER	**НЕ РАБОТАЕТ** [ne ra'bɔtaet]
CLOSED	**ЗАКРЫТО** [zak'rɪtə]

OPEN

ОТКРЫТО
[atkˈrɪtə]

FOR WOMEN

ДЛЯ ЖЕНЩИН
[dʎa ˈʒɛnɕin]

FOR MEN

ДЛЯ МУЖЧИН
[dʎa mʊˈɕin]

TOPICAL
VOCABULARY

This section contains more than 3,000 of the most important words.
The dictionary will provide invaluable assistance while traveling abroad, because frequently individual words are enough for you to be understood.
The dictionary includes a convenient transcription of each foreign word

T&P Books Publishing

VOCABULARY
CONTENTS

T&P Books Publishing

BASIC CONCEPTS

T&P Books Publishing

1. Pronouns

I, me	я	[ja]
you	ты	[tɪ]
he	он	[ɔn]
she	она	[a'na]
it	оно	[a'nɔ]
we	мы	[mɪ]
you (to a group)	вы	[vɪ]
they	они	[a'ni]

2. Greetings. Salutations

Hello! (fam.)	Здравствуй!	[zd'rastvʊj]
Hello! (form.)	Здравствуйте!	[zd'rastvʊjte]
Good morning!	Доброе утро!	['dobrae 'utra]
Good afternoon!	Добрый день!	['dobrɪj deɲ]
Good evening!	Добрый вечер!	['dobrɪj 'wetʃer]
to say hello	здороваться	[zda'rovatsə]
Hi! (hello)	Привет!	[pri'wet]
greeting (n)	привет (м)	[pri'wet]
to greet (vt)	приветствовать	[pri'wetstvavatʲ]
How are you? (form.)	Как у вас дела?	[kak u vas di'la]
How are you? (fam.)	Как дела?	[kak di'la]
What's new?	Что нового?	[ʃta 'novava]
Bye-Bye! Goodbye!	До свидания!	[da swi'danija]
See you soon!	До скорой встречи!	[da s'kɔraj fst'retʃi]
Farewell! (to a friend)	Прощай!	[pra'ɕaj]
Farewell! (form.)	Прощайте!	[pra'ɕajte]
to say goodbye	прощаться	[pra'ɕatsə]
So long!	Пока!	[pa'ka]
Thank you!	Спасибо!	[spa'siba]
Thank you very much!	Большое спасибо!	[baʎ'ʃoe spa'siba]
You're welcome	Пожалуйста	[pa'ʒalujstə]
Don't mention it!	Не стоит благодарности.	[ni s'tɔit blaga'darnasti]
It was nothing	Не за что	['ne za ʃtə]
Excuse me! (fam.)	Извини!	[izwi'ni]
Excuse me! (form.)	Извините!	[izwi'nite]

to excuse (forgive)	извинять	[izwi'natʲ]
to apologize (vi)	извиняться	[izwi'natsə]
My apologies	Мои извинения	[ma'i izwi'neniə]
I'm sorry!	Простите!	[pras'tite]
to forgive (vt)	прощать	[pra'çatʲ]
It's okay!	Ничего страшного	[nitʃi'vɔ st'raʃnavə]
please (adv)	пожалуйста	[pa'ʒalujstə]

Don't forget!	Не забудьте!	[ni za'butʲte]
Certainly!	Конечно!	[ka'neʃna]
Of course not!	Конечно нет!	[ka'neʃna 'net]
Okay! (I agree)	Согласен!	[sag'lasen]
That's enough!	Хватит!	[h'vatit]

3. Questions

Who?	Кто?	[ktɔ]
What?	Что?	[ʃtɔ]
Where? (at, in)	Где?	[gde]
Where (to)?	Куда?	[kʊ'da]
From where?	Откуда?	[at'kʊda]
When?	Когда?	[kag'da]
Why? (What for?)	Зачем?	[za'tʃem]
Why? (reason)	Почему?	[patʃe'mʊ]

What for?	Для чего?	[dʎa tʃe'vɔ]
How? (in what way)	Как?	[kak]
What? (What kind of ...?)	Какой?	[ka'kɔj]
Which?	Который?	[ka'tɔrij]

To whom?	Кому?	[ka'mʊ]
About whom?	О ком?	[a 'kɔm]
About what?	О чём?	[a 'tʃom]
With whom?	С кем?	[s kem]

How many? How much?	Сколько?	[s'kɔʎka]
Whose?	Чей?	[tʃej]
Whose? (fem.)	Чья?	[tʃja]
Whose? (pl)	Чьи?	[tʃʲi]

4. Prepositions

with (accompanied by)	с	[s]
without	без	[bes]
to (indicating direction)	в	[v]
about (talking ~ ...)	о	[ɔ]
before (in time)	перед	['peret]
in front of ...	перед	['peret]

under (beneath, below)	под	[pɔt]
above (over)	над	[nat]
on (atop)	на	[nə]
from (off, out of)	из	[is]
of (made from)	из	[is]
in (e.g., ~ ten minutes)	через	['tʃeres]
over (across the top of)	через	['tʃeres]

5. Function words. Adverbs. Part 1

Where? (at, in)	Где?	[gde]
here (adv)	здесь	[zdesʲ]
there (adv)	там	[tam]
somewhere (to be)	где-то	[g'de tə]
nowhere (not anywhere)	нигде	[nig'de]
by (near, beside)	у, около	[u], ['ɔkalə]
by the window	у окна	[u ak'na]
Where (to)?	Куда?	[kʊ'da]
here (e.g., come ~!)	сюда	[sy'da]
there (e.g., to go ~)	туда	[tʊ'da]
from here (adv)	отсюда	[a'tsydə]
from there (adv)	оттуда	[at'tʊdə]
close (adv)	близко	[b'liskə]
far (adv)	далеко	[dali'kɔ]
near (e.g., ~ Paris)	около	['ɔkalə]
nearby (adv)	рядом	['rʲadam]
not far (adv)	недалеко	[nidali'kɔ]
left (adj)	левый	['levɪj]
on the left	слева	[s'levə]
to the left	налево	[na'levə]
right (adj)	правый	[p'ravɪj]
on the right	справа	[sp'ravə]
to the right	направо	[nap'ravə]
in front (adv)	спереди	[s'peredi]
front (as adj)	передний	[pi'rednij]
ahead (the kids ran ~)	вперёд	[fpi'rɜt]
behind (adv)	сзади	[z'zadi]
from behind	сзади	[z'zadi]
back (towards the rear)	назад	[na'zat]
middle	середина (ж)	[sire'dinə]

in the middle	посередине	[pɑseri'dine]
at the side	сбоку	[z'bɔkʊ]
everywhere (adv)	везде	[wez'de]
around (in all directions)	вокруг	[vɑk'rʊk]

from inside	изнутри	[iznʊt'ri]
somewhere (to go)	куда-то	[kʊ'dɑ tə]
straight (directly)	напрямик	[nɑpri'mik]
back (e.g., come ~)	обратно	[ɑb'ratnə]

| from anywhere | откуда-нибудь | [ɑt'kʊda ni'bʊtʲ] |
| from somewhere | откуда-то | [ɑt'kʊda tə] |

firstly (adv)	во-первых	[vɑ'pervɪh]
secondly (adv)	во-вторых	[vɑfta'rɪh]
thirdly (adv)	в-третьих	[ft'retih]

suddenly (adv)	вдруг	[vdrʊk]
at first (at the beginning)	вначале	[vnɑ'ʧale]
for the first time	впервые	[fpir'vɪe]
long before ...	задолго до ...	[zɑ'dɔlga dɑ]
anew (over again)	заново	['zɑnɑvə]
for good (adv)	насовсем	[nɑsɑf'sem]

never (adv)	никогда	[nikɑg'dɑ]
again (adv)	опять	[ɑ'pʲatʲ]
now (adv)	теперь	[ti'perʲ]
often (adv)	часто	['ʧastə]
then (adv)	тогда	[tɑg'dɑ]
urgently (quickly)	срочно	[s'rɔʧnə]
usually (adv)	обычно	[ɑ'bɪʧnə]

by the way, ...	кстати, ...	[ks'tati]
possible (that is ~)	возможно	[vɑz'mɔʒnə]
probably (adv)	вероятно	[wirɑ'jatnə]
maybe (adv)	может быть	['mɔʒɛt 'bɪtʲ]
besides ...	кроме того, ...	[k'rɔme tɑ'vɔ]
that's why ...	поэтому ...	[pɑ'ɛtamʊ]
in spite of ...	несмотря на ...	[nismɑt'rʲa nɑ]
thanks to ...	благодаря ...	[blagada'rʲa]

what (pron.)	что	[ʃtɔ]
that (conj.)	что	[ʃtɔ]
something	что-то	[ʃ'tɔ tə]
anything (something)	что-нибудь	[ʃtɔ ni'bʊtʲ]
nothing	ничего	[niʧi'vɔ]

who (pron.)	кто	[ktɔ]
someone	кто-то	[k'tɔ tə]
somebody	кто-нибудь	[k'tɔ ni'bʊtʲ]
nobody	никто	[nik'tɔ]
nowhere (a voyage to ~)	никуда	[nikʊ'dɑ]

| nobody's | ничей | [ni'tʃej] |
| somebody's | чей-нибудь | [tʃej ni'butʲ] |

so (I'm ~ glad)	так	[tak]
also (as well)	также	['takʒɛ]
too (as well)	тоже	['tɔʒɛ]

6. Function words. Adverbs. Part 2

Why?	Почему?	[patʃe'mʊ]
for some reason	почему-то	[patʃe'mʊ tə]
because ...	потому, что ...	[pata'mʊʃta]
for some purpose	зачем-то	[za'tʃemtə]

and	и	[i]
or	или	['ili]
but	но	[nɔ]
for (e.g., ~ me)	для	[dʎa]

too (~ many people)	слишком	[s'liʃkam]
only (exclusively)	только	['tɔʎkə]
exactly (adv)	точно	['tɔtʃnə]
about (more or less)	около	['ɔkalə]

approximately (adv)	приблизительно	[pribli'ziteʎnə]
approximate (adj)	приблизительный	[pribli'ziteʎnɪj]
almost (adv)	почти	[patʃʲti]
the rest	остальное (c)	[astaʎ'nɔe]

each (adj)	каждый	['kaʒdɪj]
any (no matter which)	любой	[ly'bɔj]
many, much (a lot of)	много	[m'nɔgə]
many people	многие	[m'nɔgie]
all (everyone)	все	[fse]

in return for ...	в обмен на ...	[v ab'men na]
in exchange (adv)	взамен	[vza'men]
by hand (made)	вручную	[vrʊtʃ'nʊju]
hardly (negative opinion)	вряд ли	[v'rʲatli]

probably (adv)	наверное	[na'wernɑe]
on purpose (intentionally)	нарочно	[na'rɔʃnə]
by accident (adv)	случайно	[slu'tʃajnə]

very (adv)	очень	['ɔtʃəl]
for example (adv)	например	[napri'mer]
between	между	['meʒdʊ]
among	среди	[sre'di]
so much (such a lot)	столько	[s'tɔʎkə]
especially (adv)	особенно	[a'sɔbennə]

T&P BOOKS

NUMBERS.
MISCELLANEOUS

T&P Books Publishing

7.   Cardinal numbers. Part 1

0 zero	ноль	[nɔʌ]
1 one	один	[ɑ'din]
2 two	два	[dvə]
3 three	три	[tri]
4 four	четыре	[tʃi'tɪrɛ]

5 five	пять	[pʲatʲ]
6 six	шесть	[ʃəstʲ]
7 seven	семь	[semʲ]
8 eight	восемь	['vɔsemʲ]
9 nine	девять	['dewitʲ]

10 ten	десять	['desitʲ]
11 eleven	одиннадцать	[ɑ'dinɑtsatʲ]
12 twelve	двенадцать	[dwi'nɑtsatʲ]
13 thirteen	тринадцать	[tri'nɑtsatʲ]
14 fourteen	четырнадцать	[tʃi'tɪrnɑtsatʲ]

15 fifteen	пятнадцать	[pit'nɑtsatʲ]
16 sixteen	шестнадцать	[ʃɛs'nɑtsatʲ]
17 seventeen	семнадцать	[sim'nɑtsatʲ]
18 eighteen	восемнадцать	[vɑsem'nɑtsatʲ]
19 nineteen	девятнадцать	[diwit'nɑtsatʲ]

20 twenty	двадцать	[d'vɑtsatʲ]
21 twenty-one	двадцать один	[d'vɑtsatʲ ɑ'din]
22 twenty-two	двадцать два	[d'vɑtsatʲ d'va]
23 twenty-three	двадцать три	[d'vɑtsatʲ t'ri]

30 thirty	тридцать	[t'ritsatʲ]
31 thirty-one	тридцать один	[t'ritsatʲ ɑ'din]
32 thirty-two	тридцать два	[t'ritsatʲ d'va]
33 thirty-three	тридцать три	[t'ritsatʲ t'ri]

40 forty	сорок	['sɔrak]
41 forty-one	сорок один	['sɔrak ɑ'din]
42 forty-two	сорок два	['sɔrak d'va]
43 forty-three	сорок три	['sɔrak t'ri]

50 fifty	пятьдесят	[pitʲdi'sʲat]
51 fifty-one	пятьдесят один	[pitʲdi'sʲat ɑ'din]
52 fifty-two	пятьдесят два	[pitʲdi'sʲat d'va]
53 fifty-three	пятьдесят три	[pitʲdi'sʲat t'ri]
60 sixty	шестьдесят	[ʃistʲdi'sʲat]

61 sixty-one	шестьдесят один	[ʃəstʲdiˈsʲat aˈdin]
62 sixty-two	шестьдесят два	[ʃəstʲdiˈsʲat dˈva]
63 sixty-three	шестьдесят три	[ʃəstʲdiˈsʲat tˈri]

70 seventy	семьдесят	[ˈsemʲdisit]
71 seventy-one	семьдесят один	[ˈsemʲdisit aˈdin]
72 seventy-two	семьдесят два	[ˈsemʲdisit dˈva]
73 seventy-three	семьдесят три	[ˈsemʲdisit tˈri]

80 eighty	восемьдесят	[ˈvɔsemʲdisit]
81 eighty-one	восемьдесят один	[ˈvɔsemʲdisit aˈdin]
82 eighty-two	восемьдесят два	[ˈvɔsemʲdisit dˈva]
83 eighty-three	восемьдесят три	[ˈvɔsemʲdisit tˈri]

90 ninety	девяносто	[diwiˈnɔstə]
91 ninety-one	девяносто один	[diwiˈnɔsta aˈdin]
92 ninety-two	девяносто два	[diwiˈnɔsta dˈva]
93 ninety-three	девяносто три	[diwiˈnɔsta tˈri]

8. Cardinal numbers. Part 2

100 one hundred	сто	[stɔ]
200 two hundred	двести	[dˈwesti]
300 three hundred	триста	[tˈristə]
400 four hundred	четыреста	[tʃiˈtɪrestə]
500 five hundred	пятьсот	[piˈtsɔt]

600 six hundred	шестьсот	[ʃɛsˈsɔt]
700 seven hundred	семьсот	[simʲˈsɔt]
800 eight hundred	восемьсот	[vɑsemʲˈsɔt]
900 nine hundred	девятьсот	[diwiˈtsɔt]

1000 one thousand	тысяча	[ˈtɪsitʃə]
2000 two thousand	две тысячи	[dwe ˈtɪsitʃi]
3000 three thousand	три тысячи	[tri ˈtɪsitʃi]
10000 ten thousand	десять тысяч	[ˈdesitʲ ˈtɪsitʃ]
one hundred thousand	сто тысяч	[stɔ ˈtɪsitʃ]
million	миллион (м)	[miliˈɔn]
billion	миллиард (м)	[miliˈɑrt]

9. Ordinal numbers

first (adj)	первый	[ˈpervɪj]
second (adj)	второй	[ftaˈrɔj]
third (adj)	третий	[tˈretij]
fourth (adj)	четвёртый	[tʃitˈwɜrtɪj]
fifth (adj)	пятый	[ˈpʲatɪj]
sixth (adj)	шестой	[ʃɛsˈtɔj]

seventh (adj)	**седьмой**	[sidʲˈmɔj]
eighth (adj)	**восьмой**	[vɑsʲˈmɔj]
ninth (adj)	**девятый**	[dɪˈvʲatɪj]
tenth (adj)	**десятый**	[dɪˈsʲatɪj]

COLOURS. UNITS OF MEASUREMENT

T&P Books Publishing

color	цвет (м)	[tswet]
shade (tint)	оттенок (м)	[at'tenak]
hue	тон (м)	[tɔn]
rainbow	радуга (ж)	['radʊgə]
white (adj)	белый	['belɪj]
black (adj)	чёрный	['tʃɔrnɪj]
gray (adj)	серый	['serɪj]
green (adj)	зелёный	[ze'lɜnɪj]
yellow (adj)	жёлтый	['ʒɔltɪj]
red (adj)	красный	[k'rasnɪj]
blue (adj)	синий	['sinɪj]
light blue (adj)	голубой	[galu'bɔj]
pink (adj)	розовый	['rɔzavɪj]
orange (adj)	оранжевый	[a'ranʒɪvɪj]
violet (adj)	фиолетовый	[fia'letavɪj]
brown (adj)	коричневый	[ka'ritʃnevɪj]
golden (adj)	золотой	[zala'tɔj]
silvery (adj)	серебристый	[sireb'ristɪj]
beige (adj)	бежевый	['beʒɪvɪj]
cream (adj)	кремовый	[k'remavɪj]
turquoise (adj)	бирюзовый	[biry'zɔvɪj]
cherry red (adj)	вишнёвый	[wiʃ'nɜvɪj]
lilac (adj)	лиловый	[li'lovɪj]
crimson (adj)	малиновый	[ma'linavɪj]
light (adj)	светлый	[s'wetlɪj]
dark (adj)	тёмный	['tɜmnɪj]
bright, vivid (adj)	яркий	['jarkij]
colored (pencils)	цветной	[tswit'nɔj]
color (e.g., ~ film)	цветной	[tswit'nɔj]
black-and-white (adj)	чёрно-белый	['tʃɔrna 'belɪj]
plain (one-colored)	одноцветный	[adnats'wetnɪj]
multicolored (adj)	разноцветный	[raznats'wetnɪj]

weight	вес (м)	[wes]
length	длина (ж)	[dli'na]

width	ширина (ж)	[ʃɪrɪˈna]
height	высота (ж)	[vɪsaˈta]
depth	глубина (ж)	[glubɪˈna]
volume	объём (м)	[abʰˈɜm]
area	площадь (ж)	[pˈlɔçatⁱ]

gram	грамм (м)	[gram]
milligram	миллиграмм (м)	[milɪgˈram]
kilogram	килограмм (м)	[kilagˈram]
ton	тонна (ж)	[ˈtɔnnə]
pound	фунт (м)	[funt]
ounce	унция (ж)	[ˈunʦija]

meter	метр (м)	[metr]
millimeter	миллиметр (м)	[miliˈmetr]
centimeter	сантиметр (м)	[santiˈmetr]
kilometer	километр (м)	[kilaˈmetr]
mile	миля (ж)	[ˈmiʎa]

inch	дюйм (м)	[dyjm]
foot	фут (м)	[fut]
yard	ярд (м)	[ˈjart]

square meter	квадратный метр (м)	[kvadˈratnɪj metr]
hectare	гектар (м)	[gikˈtar]
liter	литр (м)	[litr]
degree	градус (м)	[gˈradus]
volt	вольт (м)	[vɔʎt]
ampere	ампер (м)	[amˈper]
horsepower	лошадиная сила (ж)	[laʃʌˈdinaja ˈsilə]

quantity	количество (с)	[kaˈlitʃestvə]
a little bit of …	немного …	[nimˈnoga]
half	половина (ж)	[palaˈwinə]
dozen	дюжина (ж)	[ˈdyʒɪnə]
piece (item)	штука (ж)	[ʃˈtukə]

| size | размер (м) | [razˈmer] |
| scale (map ~) | масштаб (м) | [maʃˈtap] |

minimal (adj)	минимальный	[miniˈmaʎnɪj]
the smallest (adj)	наименьший	[naiˈmenʃɪj]
medium (adj)	средний	[sˈrednij]
maximal (adj)	максимальный	[maksiˈmaʎnɪj]
the largest (adj)	наибольший	[naiˈbɔʎʃɪj]

12. Containers

| canning jar (glass ~) | банка (ж) | [ˈbankə] |
| can | банка (ж) | [ˈbankə] |

bucket	**ведро** (с)	[wid'rɔ]
barrel	**бочка** (ж)	['bɔʧkə]
wash basin (e.g., plastic ~)	**таз** (м)	[tɑs]
tank (100 - 200L water ~)	**бак** (м)	[bɑk]
hip flask	**фляжка** (ж)	[f'ʎaʃkə]
jerrycan	**канистра** (ж)	[ka'nistrə]
tank (e.g., tank car)	**цистерна** (ж)	[ʦɪs'ternə]
mug	**кружка** (ж)	[k'rʊʃkə]
cup (of coffee, etc.)	**чашка** (ж)	['ʧaʃkə]
saucer	**блюдце** (с)	[b'lɨʦe]
glass (tumbler)	**стакан** (м)	[stɑ'kɑn]
wine glass	**бокал** (м)	[bɑ'kɑl]
stock pot (soup pot)	**кастрюля** (ж)	[kɑst'ryʎa]
bottle (~ of wine)	**бутылка** (ж)	[bʊ'tɪlkə]
neck (of the bottle, etc.)	**горлышко** (с)	['gɔrlɨʃkə]
carafe	**графин** (м)	[grɑ'fin]
pitcher	**кувшин** (м)	[kʊf'ʃin]
vessel (container)	**сосуд** (м)	[sɑ'sʊt]
pot (crock, stoneware ~)	**горшок** (м)	[gɑr'ʃɔk]
vase	**ваза** (ж)	['vɑzə]
bottle (perfume ~)	**флакон** (м)	[flɑ'kɔn]
vial, small bottle	**пузырёк** (м)	[pʊzɪ'rɜk]
tube (of toothpaste)	**тюбик** (м)	['tybik]
sack (bag)	**мешок** (м)	[mi'ʃɔk]
bag (paper ~, plastic ~)	**пакет** (м)	[pɑ'ket]
pack (of cigarettes, etc.)	**пачка** (ж)	['paʧkə]
box (e.g., shoebox)	**коробка** (ж)	[kɑ'rɔpkə]
crate	**ящик** (м)	['jaɕik]
basket	**корзина** (ж)	[kɑr'zinə]

MAIN VERBS

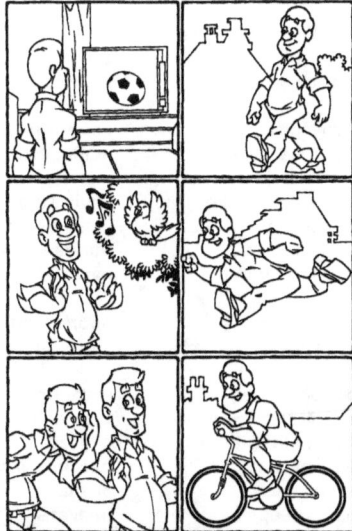

T&P Books Publishing

13. The most important verbs. Part 1

to advise (vt)	советовать	[sɑ'wetavatʲ]
to agree (say yes)	соглашаться	[sagla'ʃʌtsə]
to answer (vi, vt)	отвечать	[atwe'tʃatʲ]
to apologize (vi)	извиняться	[izwi'ɲatsə]
to arrive (vi)	приезжать	[prii'zatʲ]

to ask (~ oneself)	спрашивать	[sp'raʃivatʲ]
to ask (~ sb to do sth)	просить	[pra'sitʲ]
to be (vi)	быть	[bɪtʲ]

to be afraid	бояться	[ba'jatsə]
to be hungry	хотеть есть	[ha'tetʲ 'estʲ]
to be interested in …	интересоваться	[intirisa'vatsə]
to be needed	требоваться	[t'rebavatsə]
to be surprised	удивляться	[udiv'ʌatsə]

to be thirsty	хотеть пить	[ha'tetʲ 'pitʲ]
to begin (vt)	начинать	[natʃi'natʲ]
to belong to …	принадлежать …	[prinadle'ʒatʲ]

| to boast (vi) | хвастаться | [h'vastatsə] |
| to break (split into pieces) | ломать | [la'matʲ] |

to call (~ for help)	звать	[zvatʲ]
can (v aux)	мочь	[mɔtʃ]
to catch (vt)	ловить	[la'witʲ]

| to change (vt) | изменить | [izme'nitʲ] |
| to choose (select) | выбирать | [vɪbi'ratʲ] |

to come down (the stairs)	спускаться	[spʊs'katsə]
to compare (vt)	сравнивать	[s'ravnivatʲ]
to complain (vi, vt)	жаловаться	['ʒalavatsə]
to confuse (mix up)	путать	['pʊtatʲ]

| to continue (vt) | продолжать | [prada'ʒatʲ] |
| to control (vt) | контролировать | [kantra'liravatʲ] |

to cook (dinner)	готовить	[ga'tɔwitʲ]
to cost (vt)	стоить	[s'tɔitʲ]
to count (add up)	считать	[ɕi'tatʲ]
to count on …	рассчитывать на …	[ra'ɕitivatʲ na]
to create (vt)	создать	[saz'datʲ]
to cry (weep)	плакать	[p'lakatʲ]

14. The most important verbs. Part 2

to deceive (vi, vt)	обманывать	[ab'manivat']
to decorate (tree, street)	украшать	[ukra'ʃʌt']
to defend (a country, etc.)	защищать	[zaɕi'ɕat']
to demand (request firmly)	требовать	[t'rebavat']
to dig (vt)	рыть	[rɪt']
to discuss (vt)	обсуждать	[apsʊʒ'dat']
to do (vt)	делать	['delat']
to doubt (have doubts)	сомневаться	[samni'vatsə]
to drop (let fall)	ронять	[ra'ɲat']
to enter (room, house, etc.)	входить	[fha'dit']
to excuse (forgive)	извинять	[izwi'ɲat']
to exist (vi)	существовать	[sʊɕestva'vat']
to expect (foresee)	предвидеть	[prid'widet']
to explain (vt)	объяснять	[abʰes'ɲat']
to fall (vi)	падать	['padat']
to find (vt)	находить	[naha'dit']
to finish (vt)	заканчивать	[za'kaɲtʃivat']
to fly (vi)	лететь	[li'tet']
to follow ... (come after)	следовать за ...	[s'ledavat' za]
to forget (vi, vt)	забывать	[zabɪ'vat']
to forgive (vt)	прощать	[pra'ɕat']
to give (vt)	давать	[da'vat']
to give a hint	подсказать	[patska'zat']
to go (on foot)	идти	[it'ti]
to go for a swim	купаться	[kʊ'patsə]
to go out (for dinner, etc.)	выходить	[vɪha'dit']
to guess (the answer)	отгадать	[atga'dat']
to have (vt)	иметь	[i'met']
to have breakfast	завтракать	['zaftrakat']
to have dinner	ужинать	['uʒɪnat']
to have lunch	обедать	[a'bedat']
to hear (vt)	слышать	[s'lɪʃʌt']
to help (vt)	помогать	[pama'gat']
to hide (vt)	прятать	[p'rʲatat']
to hope (vi, vt)	надеяться	[na'deitsə]
to hunt (vi, vt)	охотиться	[a'hotitsə]
to hurry (vi)	торопиться	[tara'pitsə]

15. The most important verbs. Part 3

to inform (vt)	информировать	[infar'miravat^j]
to insist (vi, vt)	настаивать	[nas'taivat^j]
to insult (vt)	оскорблять	[askarb'ʎat^j]
to invite (vt)	приглашать	[prigla'ʃʌt^j]
to joke (vi)	шутить	[ʃu'tit^j]
to keep (vt)	сохранять	[sahra'ɲat^j]
to keep silent	молчать	[mal'ʧat^j]
to kill (vt)	убивать	[ubi'vat^j]
to know (sb)	знать	[znat^j]
to laugh (vi)	смеяться	[smi'jatsə]
to liberate (city, etc.)	освобождать	[asvabaʒ'dat^j]
to like (I like ...)	нравиться	[n'rawitsə]
to look for ... (search)	искать ...	[is'kat^j]
to love (sb)	любить	[ly'bit^j]
to make a mistake	ошибаться	[aʃi'batsə]
to manage, to run	руководить	[rukava'dit^j]
to mean (signify)	означать	[azna'ʧat^j]
to mention (talk about)	упоминать	[upami'nat^j]
to miss (school, etc.)	пропускать	[prapus'kat^j]
to notice (see)	замечать	[zame'ʧat^j]
to object (vi, vt)	возражать	[vazra'ʒat^j]
to observe (see)	наблюдать	[nably'dat^j]
to open (vt)	открывать	[atkrı'vat^j]
to order (meal, etc.)	заказывать	[za'kazıvat^j]
to order (mil.)	приказывать	[pri'kazıvat^j]
to own (possess)	владеть	[vla'det^j]
to participate (vi)	участвовать	[u'ʧastvavat^j]
to pay (vi, vt)	платить	[pla'tit^j]
to permit (vt)	разрешать	[razre'ʃʌt^j]
to plan (vt)	планировать	[pla'niravat^j]
to play (children)	играть	[ig'rat^j]
to pray (vi, vt)	молиться	[ma'litsə]
to prefer (vt)	предпочитать	[pritpaʧi'tat^j]
to promise (vt)	обещать	[abi'ɕat^j]
to pronounce (vt)	произносить	[praizna'sit^j]
to propose (vt)	предлагать	[pridla'gat^j]
to punish (vt)	наказывать	[na'kazıvat^j]

16. The most important verbs. Part 4

to read (vi, vt)	читать	[ʧi'tat^j]
to recommend (vt)	рекомендовать	[rikamenda'vat^j]

to refuse (vi, vt)	отказываться	[at'kazıvatsə]
to regret (be sorry)	сожалеть	[saʒi'letʲ]
to rent (sth from sb)	снимать	[sni'matʲ]

to repeat (say again)	повторять	[pafta'rʲatʲ]
to reserve, to book	резервировать	[rezir'wiravatʲ]
to run (vi)	бежать	[bi'ʒatʲ]
to save (rescue)	спасать	[spa'satʲ]
to say (~ thank you)	сказать	[ska'zatʲ]

to scold (vt)	ругать	[rʊ'gatʲ]
to see (vt)	видеть	['widetʲ]
to sell (vt)	продавать	[prada'vatʲ]
to send (vt)	отправлять	[atprav'ʎatʲ]
to shoot (vi)	стрелять	[stri'ʎatʲ]

to shout (vi)	кричать	[kri'ʧatʲ]
to show (vt)	показывать	[pa'kazıvatʲ]
to sign (document)	подписывать	[pat'pisıvatʲ]
to sit down (vi)	садиться	[sa'ditsə]

to smile (vi)	улыбаться	[ulı'batsə]
to speak (vi, vt)	говорить	[gava'ritʲ]
to steal (money, etc.)	красть	[krastʲ]
to stop (for pause, etc.)	останавливаться	[asta'navlivatsə]
to stop (please ~ calling me)	прекращать	[prikra'ɕatʲ]

to study (vt)	изучать	[izu'ʧatʲ]
to swim (vi)	плавать	[p'lavatʲ]
to take (vt)	брать	[bratʲ]
to think (vi, vt)	думать	['dʊmatʲ]
to threaten (vt)	угрожать	[ugra'ʒatʲ]

to touch (with hands)	трогать	[t'rɔgatʲ]
to translate (vt)	переводить	[pireva'ditʲ]
to trust (vt)	доверять	[dawe'rʲatʲ]
to try (attempt)	пробовать	[p'rɔbavatʲ]
to turn (e.g., ~ left)	поворачивать	[pava'ratʃivatʲ]

to underestimate (vt)	недооценивать	[nidaa'tsenivatʲ]
to understand (vt)	понимать	[pani'matʲ]
to unite (vt)	объединять	[abʰedi'ɲatʲ]
to wait (vt)	ждать	[ʒdatʲ]

to want (wish, desire)	хотеть	[ha'tetʲ]
to warn (vt)	предупреждать	[pridʊpreʒ'datʲ]
to work (vi)	работать	[ra'botatʲ]
to write (vt)	писать	[pi'satʲ]
to write down	записывать	[za'pisıvatʲ]

TIME. CALENDAR

T&P Books Publishing

Monday	понедельник (м)	[panɪ'deʌnɪk]
Tuesday	вторник (м)	[f'tɔrnɪk]
Wednesday	среда (ж)	[sre'da]
Thursday	четверг (м)	[ʧɪt'werk]
Friday	пятница (ж)	['pʲatnɪtsə]
Saturday	суббота (ж)	[sʊ'bɔtə]
Sunday	воскресенье (с)	[vaskrɪ'senje]
today (adv)	сегодня	[sɪ'vɔdɲa]
tomorrow (adv)	завтра	['zaftrə]
the day after tomorrow	послезавтра	[pasle'zaftrə]
yesterday (adv)	вчера	[fʧɪ'ra]
the day before yesterday	позавчера	[pazafʧe'ra]
day	день (м)	[deɲ]
working day	рабочий день (м)	[ra'bɔʧɪj deɲ]
public holiday	празник (м)	[p'raznɪk]
day off	выходной день (м)	[vɪhad'nɔj deɲ]
weekend	выходные (мн)	[vɪhad'nɪe]
all day long	весь день	[wesʲ 'deɲ]
the next day (adv)	на следующий день	[na sle'dʊɕɪj deɲ]
two days ago	2 дня назад	[dva dɲa na'zat]
the day before	накануне	[naka'nʊne]
daily (adj)	ежедневный	[eʒɪd'nevnɪj]
every day (adv)	ежедневно	[eʒɪd'nevnə]
week	неделя (ж)	[nɪ'deʌa]
last week (adv)	на прошлой неделе	[na p'rɔʃlaj nɪ'dele]
next week (adv)	на следующей неделе	[na sle'dʊɕej nɪ'dele]
weekly (adj)	еженедельный	[eʒɪnɪ'deʌnɪj]
every week (adv)	еженедельно	[eʒɪnɪ'deʌnə]
twice a week	2 раза в неделю	[dva 'raza v nɪ'dely]
every Tuesday	каждый вторник	['kaʒdɪj f'tɔrnɪk]

morning	утро (с)	['utrə]
in the morning	утром	['utram]
noon, midday	полдень (м)	['pɔldeɲ]
in the afternoon	после обеда	['pɔsle a'bedə]
evening	вечер (м)	['weʧer]

in the evening	вечером	['wetʃeram]
night	ночь (ж)	[notʃ]
at night	ночью	['notʃjy]
midnight	полночь (ж)	['polnatʃ]

second	секунда (ж)	[si'kundə]
minute	минута (ж)	[mi'nutə]
hour	час (м)	[tʃas]
half an hour	полчаса (мн)	[paltʃe'sa]
a quarter-hour	четверть (ж) часа	['tʃetwertⁱ 'tʃasə]
fifteen minutes	15 минут	[pit'natsatⁱ mi'nut]
24 hours	сутки (мн)	['sutki]

sunrise	восход (м) солнца	[vas'hot 'sontsə]
dawn	рассвет (м)	[ras'wet]
early morning	раннее утро (с)	['rannie 'utrə]
sunset	закат (м)	[za'kat]

early in the morning	рано утром	['rana 'utram]
this morning	сегодня утром	[si'vodɲa 'utram]
tomorrow morning	завтра утром	['zaftra 'utram]

this afternoon	сегодня днём	[si'vodɲa 'dnɜm]
in the afternoon	после обеда	['posle a'bedə]
tomorrow afternoon	завтра после обеда	['zaftra 'posle a'bedə]

| tonight (this evening) | сегодня вечером | [si'vodɲa 'wetʃeram] |
| tomorrow night | завтра вечером | ['zaftra 'wetʃeram] |

at 3 o'clock sharp	ровно в 3 часа	['rovna ftri tʃe'sa]
about 4 o'clock	около 4-х часов	['okala tʃetⁱ'rɜh tʃe'sof]
by 12 o'clock	к 12-ти часам	[k dwi'natsati tʃi'sam]

in 20 minutes	через 20 минут	['tʃeres d'vatsatⁱ mi'nut]
in an hour	через час	['tʃeres 'tʃas]
on time (adv)	вовремя	['vovremⁱa]

a quarter of …	без четверти …	[bes 'tʃetwerti]
within an hour	в течение часа	[f ti'tʃenii 'tʃasə]
every 15 minutes	каждые 15 минут	['kaʒdɪe pit'natsatⁱ mi'nut]
round the clock	круглые сутки	[k'ruglɪe 'sutki]

19. Months. Seasons

January	январь (м)	[en'varⁱ]
February	февраль (м)	[fiv'raʌ]
March	март (м)	[mart]
April	апрель (м)	[ap'reʌ]
May	май (м)	[maj]
June	июнь (м)	[i'juɲ]

July	июль (м)	[i'juʌ]
August	август (м)	['avgʊst]
September	сентябрь (м)	[sin'tʲabrʲ]
October	октябрь (м)	[ak'tʲabrʲ]
November	ноябрь (м)	[na'jabrʲ]
December	декабрь (м)	[di'kabrʲ]

spring	весна (ж)	[wis'na]
in spring	весной	[wis'nɔj]
spring (as adj)	весенний	[wi'sennij]

summer	лето (с)	['letə]
in summer	летом	['letam]
summer (as adj)	летний	['letnij]

fall	осень (ж)	['ɔseʌ]
in fall	осенью	['ɔseʌy]
fall (as adj)	осенний	[a'sennij]

winter	зима (ж)	[zi'ma]
in winter	зимой	[zi'mɔj]
winter (as adj)	зимний	['zimnij]

month	месяц (м)	['mesits]
this month	в этом месяце	[v 'ɛtam 'mesitsə]
next month	в следующем месяце	[f s'ledʊɕem 'mesitsə]
last month	в прошлом месяце	[f p'rɔʃlam 'mesitsə]

a month ago	месяц назад	['mesits na'zat]
in a month (a month later)	через месяц	['tʃeres 'mesits]
in 2 months (2 months later)	через 2 месяца	['tʃeres dva 'mesitsə]
the whole month	весь месяц	[wesʲ 'mesits]
all month long	целый месяц	['tselij 'mesits]

monthly (~ magazine)	ежемесячный	[eʒɪ'mesitʃnij]
monthly (adv)	ежемесячно	[eʒɪ'mesitʃnə]
every month	каждый месяц	['kaʒdij 'mesits]
twice a month	2 раза в месяц	[dva 'raza v 'mesits]

year	год (м)	[gɔt]
this year	в этом году	[v 'ɛtam ga'dʊ]
next year	в следующем году	[f s'ledʊɕem ga'dʊ]
last year	в прошлом году	[f p'rɔʃlam ga'dʊ]

a year ago	год назад	[gɔt na'zat]
in a year	через год	['tʃerez 'gɔt]
in two years	через 2 года	['tʃeres dva 'gɔdə]
the whole year	весь год	[wesʲ 'gɔt]
all year long	целый год	['tselij 'gɔt]
every year	каждый год	['kaʒdij gɔt]
annual (adj)	ежегодный	[eʒɪ'gɔdnij]

| annually (adv) | **ежегодно** | [eʒɪ'gɔdnɔ] |
| 4 times a year | **4 раза в год** | [ʧi'tɪre 'razɑ v gɔt] |

date (e.g., today's ~)	**число** (c)	[ʧis'lɔ]
date (e.g., ~ of birth)	**дата** (ж)	['datə]
calendar	**календарь** (м)	[kɑlin'dɑrʲ]

half a year	**полгода**	[pɑl'gɔdə]
six months	**полугодие** (c)	[pɑlu'gɔdie]
season (summer, etc.)	**сезон** (м)	[si'zɔn]
century	**век** (м)	[wek]

TRAVEL. HOTEL

T&P Books Publishing

tourism, travel	туризм (м)	[tʊˈrizm]
tourist	турист (м)	[tʊˈrist]
trip, voyage	путешествие (с)	[pʊteˈʃɛstwie]
adventure	приключение (с)	[priklyˈʧenie]
trip, journey	поездка (ж)	[paˈeztkə]

vacation	отпуск (м)	[ˈɔtpʊsk]
to be on vacation	быть в отпуске	[bɪtʲ v ˈɔtpʊske]
rest	отдых (м)	[ˈɔddɪh]

train	поезд (м)	[ˈpɔezt]
by train	поездом	[ˈpɔizdam]
airplane	самолёт (м)	[samaˈlɔt]
by airplane	самолётом	[samaˈlɔtam]
by car	на автомобиле	[na aftamaˈbile]
by ship	на корабле	[na karabˈle]

luggage	багаж (м)	[baˈgaʃ]
suitcase	чемодан (м)	[ʧimaˈdan]
luggage cart	тележка (ж) для багажа	[tiˈleʃka dʌa bagaˈʒa]
passport	паспорт (м)	[ˈpaspart]
visa	виза (ж)	[ˈwizə]
ticket	билет (м)	[biˈlet]
air ticket	авиабилет (м)	[awiabiˈlet]

guidebook	путеводитель (м)	[pʊtevaˈditeʌ]
map (tourist ~)	карта (ж)	[ˈkartə]
area (rural ~)	местность (ж)	[ˈmesnastʲ]
place, site	место (с)	[ˈmestə]

exotica (n)	экзотика (ж)	[ɛkˈzɔtikə]
exotic (adj)	экзотический	[ɛkzaˈtiʧeskij]
amazing (adj)	удивительный	[udiˈwiteʌnɪj]

group	группа (ж)	[gˈrʊpə]
excursion, sightseeing tour	экскурсия (ж)	[ɛksˈkʊrsija]
guide (person)	экскурсовод (м)	[ɛkskʊrsaˈvɔt]

| hotel | гостиница (ж) | [gasˈtinitsə] |
| motel | мотель (м) | [maˈteʌ] |

three-star	3 звезды	[tri zwez'dı]
five-star	5 звёзд	[pʲatʲ ˈzwɜst]
to stay (in hotel, etc.)	остановиться	[astana'witsə]

room	номер (м)	['nɔmer]
single room	одноместный номер (м)	[adna'mesnıj 'nɔmer]
double room	двухместный номер (м)	[dvʊh'mesnıj 'nɔmer]
to book a room	бронировать номер	[bra'niravatʲ 'nɔmer]

| half board | полупансион (м) | [palupansi'ɔn] |
| full board | полный пансион (м) | ['pɔlnıj pansi'ɔn] |

with bath	с ванной	[s 'vannaj]
with shower	с душем	[s 'duʃəm]
satellite television	спутниковое телевидение (с)	[s'pʊtnikavae tele'widenie]

air-conditioner	кондиционер (м)	[kanditsıa'ner]
towel	полотенце (с)	[pala'tentse]
key	ключ (м)	[klyʧ]

administrator	администратор (м)	[administ'ratar]
chambermaid	горничная (ж)	['gɔrnitʃnaja]
porter, bellboy	носильщик (м)	[na'siʎɕik]
doorman	портье (с)	[par'tʲe]

restaurant	ресторан (м)	[rista'ran]
pub, bar	бар (м)	[bar]
breakfast	завтрак (м)	['zaftrak]
dinner	ужин (м)	['uʒın]
buffet	шведский стол (м)	[ʃ'wetskij s'tɔl]

| lobby | вестибюль (м) | [wisti'byʎ] |
| elevator | лифт (м) | [lift] |

| DO NOT DISTURB | НЕ БЕСПОКОИТЬ | [ni bespa'kɔitʲ] |
| NO SMOKING | НЕ КУРИТЬ! | [ni kʊ'ritʲ] |

22. Sightseeing

monument	памятник (м)	['pamitnik]
fortress	крепость (ж)	[k'repastʲ]
palace	дворец (м)	[dva'rets]
castle	замок (м)	['zamak]
tower	башня (ж)	['baʃna]
mausoleum	мавзолей (м)	[mavza'lej]

architecture	архитектура (ж)	[arhitek'tʊrə]
medieval (adj)	средневековый	[sredniwi'kovıj]
ancient (adj)	старинный	[sta'rinnıj]
national (adj)	национальный	[natsıa'naʎnıj]

well-known (adj)	**известный**	[iz'wesnɪj]
tourist	**турист** (м)	[tʊ'rist]
guide (person)	**гид** (м)	[git]
excursion, sightseeing tour	**экскурсия** (ж)	[ɛks'kʊrsija]
to show (vt)	**показывать**	[pɑ'kɑzɪvatʲ]
to tell (vt)	**рассказывать**	[rɑs'kɑzɪvatʲ]
to find (vt)	**найти**	[nɑj'ti]
to get lost (lose one's way)	**потеряться**	[pɑti'rʲatsə]
map (e.g., subway ~)	**схема** (ж)	[s'hemə]
map (e.g., city ~)	**план** (м)	[plɑn]
souvenir, gift	**сувенир** (м)	[sʊwe'nir]
gift shop	**магазин** (м) **сувениров**	[mɑgɑ'zin sʊwe'nirɑf]
to take pictures	**фотографировать**	[fɑtɑgrɑ'firɑvatʲ]
to have one's picture taken	**фотографироваться**	[fɑtɑgrɑ'firɑvɑtsə]

T&P BOOKS

TRANSPORTATION

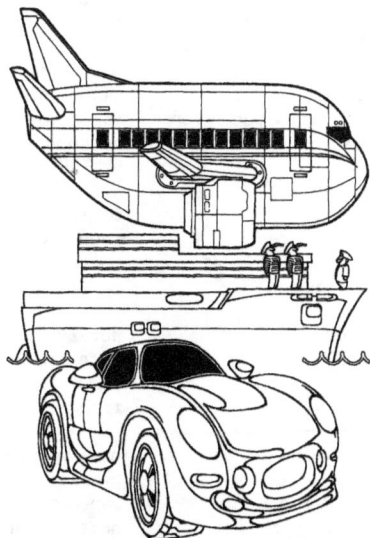

T&P Books Publishing

airport	аэропорт (м)	[aəra'pɔrt]
airplane	самолёт (м)	[sama'lɜt]
airline	авиакомпания (ж)	[awiakam'panija]
air traffic controller	диспетчер (м)	[dis'petʃer]
departure	вылет (м)	['vɪlet]
arrival	прилёт (м)	[pri'lɜt]
to arrive (by plane)	прилететь	[prile'tetʲ]
departure time	время (с) вылета	[v'remʲa 'vɪletə]
arrival time	время (с) прилёта	[v'remʲa pri'lɜtə]
to be delayed	задерживаться	[za'derʒɪvatsə]
flight delay	задержка (ж) вылета	[za'derʃka 'vɪletə]
information board	информационное табло (с)	[infarmatsɪ'ɔnɑe tab'lɔ]
information	информация (ж)	[infar'matsɪja]
to announce (vt)	объявлять	[abʰiv'ʎatʲ]
flight (e.g., next ~)	рейс (м)	[rejs]
customs	таможня (ж)	[ta'mɔʒna]
customs officer	таможенник (м)	[ta'mɔʒɛnik]
customs declaration	декларация (ж)	[dikla'ratsija]
to fill out (vt)	заполнить	[za'pɔlnitʲ]
to fill out the declaration	заполнить декларацию	[za'pɔlnitʲ dekla'ratsiju]
passport control	паспортный контроль (м)	['paspartnɪj kant'rɔʎ]
luggage	багаж (м)	[ba'gaʃ]
hand luggage	ручная кладь (ж)	[rʊtʲʰnaja klatʲ]
Lost Luggage Desk	розыск (м) багажа	['rɔzɪsk baga'ʒa]
luggage cart	тележка (ж) для багажа	[ti'leʃka dʎa baga'ʒa]
landing	посадка (ж)	[pa'satkə]
landing strip	посадочная полоса (ж)	[pa'sadatʃnaja pala'sa]
to land (vi)	садиться	[sa'ditsə]
airstairs	трап (м)	[trap]
check-in	регистрация (ж)	[regist'ratsɪja]
check-in desk	стойка (ж) регистрации	[s'tɔjka regist'ratsii]
to check-in (vi)	зарегистрироваться	[zaregist'riravatsə]
boarding pass	посадочный талон (м)	[pa'sadatʃnɪj ta'lɔn]

departure gate	выход (м)	['vıhat]
transit	транзит (м)	[tran'zit]
to wait (vt)	ждать	[ʒdatʲ]
departure lounge	зал (м) ожидания	[zal aʒı'danija]
to see off	провожать	[prava'ʒatʲ]
to say goodbye	прощаться	[pra'çatsə]

24. Airplane

airplane	самолёт (м)	[sama'lзt]
air ticket	авиабилет (м)	[awiabi'let]
airline	авиакомпания (ж)	[awiakam'panija]
airport	аэропорт (м)	[aəra'pɔrt]
supersonic (adj)	сверхзвуковой	[swerhzvʊka'vɔj]

captain	командир (м) корабля	[kaman'dir karab'ʎa]
crew	экипаж (м)	[ɛki'paʃ]
pilot	пилот (м)	[pi'lɔt]
flight attendant	стюардесса (ж)	[styar'desə]
navigator	штурман (м)	[ʃ'tʊrman]

wings	крылья (с мн)	[k'rıʎja]
tail	хвост (м)	[hvɔst]
cockpit	кабина (ж)	[ka'binə]
engine	двигатель (м)	[d'wigateʎ]
undercarriage (landing gear)	шасси (с)	[ʃʌ'si]
turbine	турбина (ж)	[tʊr'binə]

propeller	пропеллер (м)	[pra'peler]
black box	чёрный ящик (м)	['tʃɔrnıj 'jaçik]
yoke (control column)	штурвал (м)	[ʃtʊr'val]
fuel	горючее (с)	[ga'rytʃee]

safety card	инструкция по безопасности	[inst'rʊktsija pɔ biza'pasnɔsti]
oxygen mask	кислородная маска (ж)	[kisla'rɔdnaja 'maskə]
uniform	униформа (ж)	[uni'fɔrmə]
life vest	спасательный жилет (м)	[spa'sateʎnıj ʒı'let]
parachute	парашют (м)	[para'ʃyt]

takeoff	взлёт (м)	['vzlзt]
to take off (vi)	взлетать	[vzle'tatʲ]
runway	взлётная полоса (ж)	['vzlзtnaja pala'sa]

visibility	видимость (ж)	['widimastʲ]
flight (act of flying)	полёт (м)	[pa'lзt]
altitude	высота (ж)	[vısa'ta]
air pocket	воздушная яма (ж)	[vaz'dʊʃnaja 'jamə]
seat	место (с)	['mestə]

headphones	наушники (м мн)	[na'uʃniki]
folding tray (tray table)	откидной столик (м)	[atkid'nɔj s'tɔlik]
airplane window	иллюминатор (м)	[ilymi'natar]
aisle	проход (м)	[pra'hɔt]

25. Train

train	поезд (м)	['pɔezt]
commuter train	электричка (ж)	[ɛlekt'ritʃkə]
express train	скорый поезд (м)	[s'kɔrij 'pɔezt]
diesel locomotive	тепловоз (м)	[tepla'vɔs]
steam locomotive	паровоз (м)	[para'vɔs]

| passenger car | вагон (м) | [va'gɔn] |
| dining car | вагон-ресторан (м) | [va'gɔn resta'ran] |

rails	рельсы (мн)	['reʌsɨ]
railroad	железная дорога (ж)	[ʒɛ'leznaja da'rɔgə]
railway tie	шпала (ж)	[ʃ'palə]

platform (railway ~)	платформа (ж)	[plat'fɔrmə]
track (~ 1, 2, etc.)	путь (м)	[pʊtʲ]
semaphore	семафор (м)	[sima'fɔr]
station	станция (ж)	[s'tantsija]

engineer (train driver)	машинист (м)	[maʃɨ'nist]
porter (of luggage)	носильщик (м)	[na'siʌɕik]
car attendant	проводник (м)	[pravad'nik]
passenger	пассажир (м)	[pasa'ʒir]
conductor (ticket inspector)	контролёр (м)	[kantra'lɜr]

| corridor (in train) | коридор (м) | [kari'dɔr] |
| emergency brake | стоп-кран (м) | [stɔp k'ran] |

compartment	купе (с)	[kʊ'pɛ]
berth	полка (ж)	['pɔlkə]
upper berth	верхняя полка (ж)	['werhnija 'pɔlkə]
lower berth	нижняя полка (ж)	['niʒnija 'pɔlkə]
bed linen, bedding	постельное бельё (с)	[pas'teʌnae be'ʌjo]

ticket	билет (м)	[bi'let]
schedule	расписание (с)	[raspi'sanie]
information display	табло (с)	[tab'lɔ]

to leave, to depart	отходить	[atha'ditʲ]
departure (of train)	отправление (с)	[atprav'lenie]
to arrive (ab. train)	прибывать	[pribɨ'vatʲ]
arrival	прибытие (с)	[pri'bɨtie]
to arrive by train	приехать поездом	[pri'ehatʲ 'pɔizdam]

| to get on the train | сесть на поезд | [sestʲ na 'poezt] |
| to get off the train | сойти с поезда | [saj'ti s 'poezdə] |

| train wreck | крушение (с) | [kru'ʃənie] |
| to derail (vi) | сойти с рельс | [saj'ti s reʌs] |

steam locomotive	паровоз (м)	[para'vos]
stoker, fireman	кочегар (м)	[katʃe'gar]
firebox	топка (ж)	['topkə]
coal	уголь (м)	['ugaʌ]

26. Ship

| ship | корабль (м) | [ka'rabʌ] |
| vessel | судно (с) | ['sudnə] |

steamship	пароход (м)	[para'hot]
riverboat	теплоход (м)	[tipla'hot]
cruise ship	лайнер (м)	['lajner]
cruiser	крейсер (м)	[k'rejser]

yacht	яхта (ж)	['jahtə]
tugboat	буксир (м)	[buk'sir]
barge	баржа (ж)	['barʒə]
ferry	паром (м)	[pa'rom]

| sailing ship | парусник (м) | ['parusnik] |
| brigantine | бригантина (ж) | [brigan'tinə] |

| ice breaker | ледокол (м) | [lida'kol] |
| submarine | подводная лодка (ж) | [pad'vodnaja 'lotkə] |

boat (flat-bottomed ~)	лодка (ж)	['lotkə]
dinghy	шлюпка (ж)	[ʃ'lypkə]
lifeboat	спасательная шлюпка (ж)	[spa'sateʌnaja ʃ'lypkə]
motorboat	катер (м)	['kater]

captain	капитан (м)	[kapi'tan]
seaman	матрос (м)	[mat'ros]
sailor	моряк (м)	[ma'rʲak]
crew	экипаж (м)	[ɛki'paʃ]

boatswain	боцман (м)	['botsman]
ship's boy	юнга (м)	['juhgə]
cook	кок (м)	[kok]
ship's doctor	судовой врач (м)	[suda'voj vratʃ]

| deck | палуба (ж) | ['palubə] |
| mast | мачта (ж) | ['matʃtə] |

sail	парус (м)	['parʊs]
hold	трюм (м)	[trym]
bow (prow)	нос (м)	[nɔs]
stern	корма (ж)	[kar'ma]
oar	весло (с)	[wis'lɔ]
screw propeller	винт (м)	[wint]

cabin	каюта (ж)	[ka'jutə]
wardroom	кают-компания (ж)	[ka'jut kam'panija]
engine room	машинное отделение (с)	[ma'ʃinnae atde'lenie]
bridge	капитанский мостик (м)	[kapi'tanskij 'mɔstik]
radio room	радиорубка (ж)	[radia'rʊpkə]
wave (radio)	волна (ж)	[val'na]
logbook	судовой журнал (м)	[sʊda'vɔj ʒʊr'nal]

spyglass	подзорная труба (ж)	[pa'dzɔrnaja trʊ'ba]
bell	колокол (м)	['kɔlakal]
flag	флаг (м)	[flak]

| rope (mooring ~) | канат (м) | [ka'nat] |
| knot (bowline, etc.) | узел (м) | ['uzel] |

| deckrails | поручень (м) | ['pɔrʊtʃeɲ] |
| gangway | трап (м) | [trap] |

anchor	якорь (м)	['jakarʲ]
to weigh anchor	поднять якорь	[pad'natʲ 'jakarʲ]
to drop anchor	бросить якорь	[b'rɔsitʲ 'jakarʲ]
anchor chain	якорная цепь (ж)	['jakarnaja 'tsepʲ]

port (harbor)	порт (м)	[pɔrt]
quay, wharf	причал (м)	[pri'tʃal]
to berth (moor)	причаливать	[pri'tʃalivatʲ]
to cast off	отчаливать	[a'tʃalivatʲ]

trip, voyage	путешествие (с)	[pʊte'ʃɛstwie]
cruise (sea trip)	круиз (м)	[krʊ'is]
course (route)	курс (м)	[kʊrs]
route (itinerary)	маршрут (м)	[marʃ'rʊt]

fairway	фарватер (м)	[far'vater]
shallows	мель (ж)	[meʎ]
to run aground	сесть на мель	[sestʲ na 'meʎ]

storm	буря (ж)	['bʊrʲa]
signal	сигнал (м)	[sig'nal]
to sink (vi)	тонуть	[ta'nʊtʲ]
Man overboard!	Человек за бортом!	[tʃela'wek za 'bɔrtam]
SOS (distress signal)	SOS (м)	[sɔs]
ring buoy	спасательный круг (м)	[spa'sateʎnɪj krʊk]

T&P BOOKS

CITY

T&P Books Publishing

27. Urban transportation

bus	автобус (м)	[af'tɔbʊs]
streetcar	трамвай (м)	[tram'vaj]
trolley bus	троллейбус (м)	[tra'lejbʊs]
route (of bus, etc.)	маршрут (м)	[marʃ'rʊt]
number (e.g., bus ~)	номер (м)	['nɔmer]

to go by ...	ехать на ...	['ehatʲ na]
to get on (~ the bus)	сесть на ...	[sestʲ na]
to get off ...	сойти с ...	[saj'ti s]

stop (e.g., bus ~)	остановка (ж)	[asta'nɔfkə]
next stop	следующая остановка (ж)	[s'ledʊɕaja asta'nɔfkə]
terminus	конечная остановка (ж)	[ka'netʃnaja asta'nɔfkə]
schedule	расписание (с)	[raspi'sanie]
to wait (vt)	ждать	[ʒdatʲ]

| ticket | билет (м) | [bi'let] |
| fare | стоимость (ж) билета | [s'tɔimastʲ bi'letə] |

cashier (ticket seller)	кассир (м)	[kas'sir]
ticket inspection	контроль (м)	[kant'rɔʎ]
ticket inspector	контролёр (м)	[kantra'lɜr]

to be late (for ...)	опаздывать на ...	[a'pazdɪvatʲ na]
to miss (~ the train, etc.)	опоздать на ...	[apaz'datʲ na]
to be in a hurry	спешить	[spi'ʃitʲ]

taxi, cab	такси (с)	[tak'si]
taxi driver	таксист (м)	[tak'sist]
by taxi	на такси	[na tak'si]
taxi stand	стоянка (ж) такси	[sta'janka tak'si]
to call a taxi	вызвать такси	['vɪzvatʲ tak'si]
to take a taxi	взять такси	[vzʲatʲ tak'si]

traffic	уличное движение (с)	['ulitʃnae dwi'ʒɛnie]
traffic jam	пробка (ж)	[p'rɔpkə]
rush hour	часы пик (м)	[tʃə'sɪ pik]
to park (vi)	парковаться	[parka'vatsə]
to park (vt)	парковать	[parka'vatʲ]
parking lot	стоянка (ж)	[sta'jankə]

| subway | метро (с) | [mit'rɔ] |
| station | станция (ж) | [s'tantsɪja] |

to take the subway	ехать на метро	['ehat^j na met'rɔ]
train	поезд (м)	['pɔezt]
train station	вокзал (м)	[vak'zal]

28. City. Life in the city

city, town	город (м)	['gɔrat]
capital city	столица (ж)	[sta'litsə]
village	деревня (ж)	[di'revɲa]

city map	план (м) города	[plan 'gɔradə]
downtown	центр (м) города	[tsɛntr 'gɔradə]
suburb	пригород (м)	[p'rigarat]
suburban (adj)	пригородный	[p'rigaradnɪj]

outskirts	окраина (ж)	[ak'rainə]
environs (suburbs)	окрестности (ж мн)	[ak'resnasti]
city block	квартал (м)	[kvar'tal]
residential block (area)	жилой квартал (м)	[ʒɪ'lɔj kvar'tal]

traffic	движение (с)	[dwi'ʒɛnie]
traffic lights	светофор (м)	[swita'fɔr]
public transportation	городской транспорт (м)	[garats'kɔj t'ranspart]
intersection	перекрёсток (м)	[pirek'rɜstak]

crosswalk	переход (м)	[pere'hɔt]
pedestrian underpass	подземный переход (м)	[pa'dzemnɪj pere'hɔt]
to cross (~ the street)	переходить	[pereha'dit^j]
pedestrian	пешеход (м)	[piʃe'hɔt]
sidewalk	тротуар (м)	[tratʊ'ar]

bridge	мост (м)	[mɔst]
embankment (river walk)	набережная (ж)	['nabereʒnaja]
fountain	фонтан (м)	[fan'tan]

allée (garden walkway)	аллея (ж)	[a'leja]
park	парк (м)	[park]
boulevard	бульвар (м)	[bʊʎ'var]
square	площадь (ж)	[p'lɔɕat^j]
avenue (wide street)	проспект (м)	[pras'pekt]
street	улица (ж)	['ulitsə]
side street	переулок (м)	[pire'ulak]
dead end	тупик (м)	[tʊ'pik]

house	дом (м)	[dɔm]
building	здание (с)	[z'danie]
skyscraper	небоскрёб (м)	[nibask'rɜp]

| facade | фасад (м) | [fa'sat] |
| roof | крыша (ж) | [k'rɪʃə] |

window	окно (с)	[ak'nɔ]
arch	арка (ж)	['arkə]
column	колонна (ж)	[ka'lɔnnə]
corner	угол (м)	['ugal]

store window	витрина (ж)	[wit'rinə]
signboard (store sign, etc.)	вывеска (ж)	['vıwiskə]
poster	афиша (ж)	[a'fiʃə]
advertising poster	рекламный плакат (м)	[rek'lamnıj pla'kat]
billboard	рекламный щит (м)	[rek'lamnıj ɕit]

garbage, trash	мусор (м)	['mʊsar]
trashcan (public ~)	урна (ж)	['urnə]
to litter (vi)	сорить	[sa'rit']
garbage dump	свалка (ж)	[s'valkə]

phone booth	телефонная будка (ж)	[tele'fɔnnaja 'bʊtkə]
lamppost	фонарный столб (м)	[fa'narnıj s'tɔlp]
bench (park ~)	скамейка (ж)	[ska'mejkə]

police officer	полицейский (м)	[pali'tsəjskij]
police	полиция (ж)	[pa'litsıja]
beggar	нищий (м)	['niɕij]
homeless (n)	бездомный (м)	[biz'dɔmnıj]

29. Urban institutions

store	магазин (м)	[maga'zin]
drugstore, pharmacy	аптека (ж)	[ap'tekə]
eyeglass store	оптика (ж)	['ɔptikə]
shopping mall	торговый центр (м)	[tar'gɔvıj tsəntr]
supermarket	супермаркет (м)	[sʊper'market]

bakery	булочная (ж)	['bʊlatʃnaja]
baker	пекарь (м)	['pekar']
candy store	кондитерская (ж)	[kan'diterskaja]
grocery store	бакалея (ж)	[baka'leja]
butcher shop	мясная лавка (ж)	[m'as'naja 'lafkə]

| produce store | овощная лавка (ж) | [avaɕ'naja 'lafkə] |
| market | рынок (м) | ['rınak] |

coffee house	кафе (с)	[ka'fɛ]
restaurant	ресторан (м)	[rista'ran]
pub, bar	пивная (ж)	[piv'naja]
pizzeria	пиццерия (ж)	[pitsı'rija]

hair salon	парикмахерская (ж)	[parih'maherskaja]
post office	почта (ж)	['pɔtʃtə]
dry cleaners	химчистка (ж)	[him'tʃistkə]

photo studio	фотоателье (с)	[fɔtaatɛ'ʎje]
shoe store	обувной магазин (м)	[abʊv'nɔj maga'zin]
bookstore	книжный магазин (м)	[k'niʒnɪj maga'zin]
sporting goods store	спортивный магазин (м)	[spar'tivnɪj maga'zin]

clothes repair shop	ремонт (м) одежды	[re'mɔnt a'deʒdɪ]
formal wear rental	прокат (м) одежды	[pra'kat a'deʒdɪ]
video rental store	прокат (м) фильмов	[pra'kat 'fiʎmaf]

circus	цирк (м)	[tsɪrk]
zoo	зоопарк (м)	[zaa'park]
movie theater	кинотеатр (м)	[kinati'atr]
museum	музей (м)	[mʊ'zej]
library	библиотека (ж)	[biblia'tekə]

theater	театр (м)	[ti'atr]
opera (opera house)	опера (ж)	['ɔperə]
nightclub	ночной клуб (м)	[natʃ'nɔj klup]
casino	казино (с)	[kazi'nɔ]

mosque	мечеть (ж)	[mi'tʃetʲ]
synagogue	синагога (ж)	[sina'gɔgə]
cathedral	собор (м)	[sa'bɔr]
temple	храм (м)	[hram]
church	церковь (ж)	['tsərkafʲ]

college	институт (м)	[insti'tʊt]
university	университет (м)	[uniwersi'tet]
school	школа (ж)	[ʃ'kɔlə]

prefecture	префектура (ж)	[prifek'tʊrə]
city hall	мэрия (ж)	['mɛrija]
hotel	гостиница (ж)	[gas'tinitsə]
bank	банк (м)	[bank]

embassy	посольство (с)	[pa'sɔʎstvə]
travel agency	турагентство (с)	[tʊra'genstvə]
information office	справочное бюро (с)	[sp'ravatʃnae by'rɔ]
currency exchange	обменный пункт (м)	[ab'mennɪj pʊnkt]

| subway | метро (с) | [mit'rɔ] |
| hospital | больница (ж) | [baʎ'nitsə] |

| gas station | бензозаправка (ж) | [binzazap'rafkə] |
| parking lot | стоянка (ж) | [sta'jankə] |

30. Signs

| signboard (store sign, etc.) | вывеска (ж) | ['vɪwiskə] |
| notice (door sign, etc.) | надпись (ж) | ['natpisʲ] |

poster	плакат (м)	[pla'kat]
direction sign	указатель (м)	[uka'zateʎ]
arrow (sign)	стрелка (ж)	[st'relkə]
caution	предостережение (с)	[pridastire'ʒenie]
warning sign	предупреждение (с)	[pridʊpriʒ'denie]
to warn (vt)	предупредить	[pridʊpre'ditʲ]
rest day (weekly ~)	выходной день (м)	[vɪhad'nɔj deɲ]
timetable (schedule)	расписание (с)	[raspi'sanie]
opening hours	часы (мн) работы	[ʧa'sɪ ra'bɔtɪ]
WELCOME!	ДОБРО ПОЖАЛОВАТЬ!	[dab'rɔ pa'ʒalavatʲ]
ENTRANCE	ВХОД	[vhɔt]
EXIT	ВЫХОД	['vɪhat]
PUSH	ОТ СЕБЯ	[at se'bʲa]
PULL	НА СЕБЯ	[na se'bʲa]
OPEN	ОТКРЫТО	[atk'rɪtə]
CLOSED	ЗАКРЫТО	[zak'rɪtə]
WOMEN	ДЛЯ ЖЕНЩИН	[dʎa 'ʒɛɳɕin]
MEN	ДЛЯ МУЖЧИН	[dʎa mʊ'ɕin]
DISCOUNTS	СКИДКИ	[s'kitki]
SALE	РАСПРОДАЖА	[raspra'daʒə]
NEW!	НОВИНКА!	[na'winkə]
FREE	БЕСПЛАТНО	[bisp'latnə]
ATTENTION!	ВНИМАНИЕ!	[vni'manie]
NO VACANCIES	МЕСТ НЕТ	[mest 'net]
RESERVED	ЗАРЕЗЕРВИРОВАНО	[zarizir'wiravanə]
ADMINISTRATION	АДМИНИСТРАЦИЯ	[administ'ratsɪja]
STAFF ONLY	ТОЛЬКО ДЛЯ ПЕРСОНАЛА	['tɔʎka dʎa persa'nalə]
BEWARE OF THE DOG!	ЗЛАЯ СОБАКА	[z'laja sa'bakə]
NO SMOKING	НЕ КУРИТЬ!	[ni kʊ'ritʲ]
DO NOT TOUCH!	РУКАМИ НЕ ТРОГАТЬ!	[rʊ'kami ni t'rɔgatʲ]
DANGEROUS	ОПАСНО	[a'pasnə]
DANGER	ОПАСНОСТЬ	[a'pasnastʲ]
HIGH VOLTAGE	ВЫСОКОЕ НАПРЯЖЕНИЕ	[vɪ'sɔkae napri'ʒenie]
NO SWIMMING!	КУПАТЬСЯ ЗАПРЕЩЕНО	[kʊ'patsa zapreɕe'nɔ]
OUT OF ORDER	НЕ РАБОТАЕТ	[ni ra'bɔtaet]
FLAMMABLE	ОГНЕОПАСНО	[agnea'pasnə]
FORBIDDEN	ЗАПРЕЩЕНО	[zapreɕe'nɔ]
NO TRESPASSING!	ПРОХОД ЗАПРЕЩЁН	[pra'hɔd zapri'ɕɜn]
WET PAINT	ОКРАШЕНО	[ak'raʃinə]

31. Shopping

to buy (purchase)	покупать	[paku'patʲ]
purchase	покупка (ж)	[pa'kupkə]
to go shopping	делать покупки	['delatʲ pa'kupki]
shopping	шоппинг (м)	['ʃɔpink]

| to be open (ab. store) | работать | [ra'botatʲ] |
| to be closed | закрыться | [zak'rɪtsə] |

footwear, shoes	обувь (ж)	['ɔbufʲ]
clothes, clothing	одежда (ж)	[a'deʒdə]
cosmetics	косметика (ж)	[kas'metikə]
food products	продукты (мн)	[pra'duktɪ]
gift, present	подарок (м)	[pa'darak]

| salesman | продавец (м) | [prada'wets] |
| saleswoman | продавщица (ж) | [pradafɕitsə] |

check out, cash desk	касса (ж)	['kassə]
mirror	зеркало (с)	['zerkalə]
counter (store ~)	прилавок (м)	[pri'lavak]
fitting room	примерочная (ж)	[pri'meratʃnaja]

to try on	примерить	[pri'meritʲ]
to fit (ab. dress, etc.)	подходить	[padha'ditʲ]
to like (I like ...)	нравиться	[n'rawitsə]

price	цена (ж)	[tsɪ'na]
price tag	ценник (м)	['tsɛnnik]
to cost (vt)	стоить	[s'toitʲ]
How much?	Сколько?	[s'kɔʎka]
discount	скидка (ж)	[s'kitkə]

inexpensive (adj)	недорогой	[nidara'gɔj]
cheap (adj)	дешёвый	[di'ʃɔvɪj]
expensive (adj)	дорогой	[dara'gɔj]
It's expensive	Это дорого.	['ɛta 'dɔragə]

rental (n)	прокат (м)	[pra'kat]
to rent (~ a tuxedo)	взять напрокат	[vzʲatʲ napra'kat]
credit (trade credit)	кредит (м)	[kri'dit]
on credit (adv)	в кредит	[f kre'dit]

CLOTHING & ACCESSORIES

T&P Books Publishing

32. Outerwear. Coats

clothes	одежда (ж)	[a'deʒdə]
outerwear	верхняя одежда (ж)	['werhnija a'deʒdə]
winter clothing	зимняя одежда (ж)	['zimɲaja a'deʒdə]

coat (overcoat)	пальто (с)	[paʎ'tɔ]
fur coat	шуба (ж)	['ʃubə]
fur jacket	полушубок (м)	[palu'ʃubak]
down coat	пуховик (м)	[puha'wik]

jacket (e.g., leather ~)	куртка (ж)	['kurtkə]
raincoat (trenchcoat, etc.)	плащ (м)	[plaɕ]
waterproof (adj)	непромокаемый	[niprama'kaemɪj]

33. Men's & women's clothing

shirt (button shirt)	рубашка (ж)	[ru'baʃkə]
pants	брюки (мн)	[b'ryki]
jeans	джинсы (мн)	['dʒinsɪ]
suit jacket	пиджак (м)	[pi'dʒak]
suit	костюм (м)	[kas'tym]

dress (frock)	платье (с)	[p'latje]
skirt	юбка (ж)	['jupkə]
blouse	блузка (ж)	[b'luskə]
knitted jacket (cardigan, etc.)	кофта (ж)	['kɔftə]
jacket (of woman's suit)	жакет (м)	[ʒe'ket]

T-shirt	футболка (ж)	[fud'bɔlkə]
shorts (short trousers)	шорты (мн)	['ʃɔrtɪ]
tracksuit	спортивный костюм (м)	[spar'tivnɪj kas'tym]
bathrobe	халат (м)	[ha'lat]
pajamas	пижама (ж)	[pi'ʒamə]

| sweater | свитер (м) | [s'witer] |
| pullover | пуловер (м) | [pu'lɔwer] |

vest	жилет (м)	[ʒɪ'let]
tailcoat	фрак (м)	[frak]
tuxedo	смокинг (м)	[s'mɔkink]
uniform	форма (ж)	['fɔrmə]
workwear	рабочая одежда (ж)	[ra'bɔtʃija a'deʒdə]

| overalls | комбинезон (м) | [kʌmbini'zɔn] |
| coat (e.g., doctor's smock) | халат (м) | [ha'lat] |

34. Clothing. Underwear

underwear	бельё (с)	[bi'ʎjo]
boxers	трусы (м)	[trʊ'sɪ]
panties	бельё (с)	[bi'ʎjo]
undershirt (A-shirt)	майка (ж)	['majkə]
socks	носки (мн)	[nɑs'ki]

nightgown	ночная рубашка (ж)	[natʃ'naja rʊ'baʃkə]
bra	бюстгальтер (м)	[bys'gaʎtɛr]
knee highs (knee-high socks)	гольфы (мн)	['gɔʎfɪ]
pantyhose	колготки (мн)	[kal'gɔtki]
stockings (thigh highs)	чулки (мн)	[tʃul'ki]
bathing suit	купальник (м)	[kʊ'paʎnik]

35. Headwear

hat	шапка (ж)	['ʃʌpkə]
fedora	шляпа (ж)	[ʃ'ʎapə]
baseball cap	бейсболка (ж)	[bijz'bɔlkə]
flatcap	кепка (ж)	['kepkə]

beret	берет (м)	[bi'ret]
hood	капюшон (м)	[kapy'ʃɔn]
panama hat	панамка (ж)	[pa'namkə]
knit cap (knitted hat)	вязаная шапочка (ж)	['vʲazanaja 'ʃʌpatʃkə]

| headscarf | платок (м) | [pla'tɔk] |
| women's hat | шляпка (ж) | [ʃ'ʎapkə] |

hard hat	каска (ж)	['kaskə]
garrison cap	пилотка (ж)	[pi'lɔtkə]
helmet	шлем (м)	[ʃlem]

| derby | котелок (м) | [kate'lɔk] |
| top hat | цилиндр (м) | [tsɪ'lindr] |

36. Footwear

footwear	обувь (ж)	['ɔbʊfʲ]
shoes (men's shoes)	ботинки (мн)	[ba'tinki]
shoes (women's shoes)	туфли (мн)	['tʊfli]

| boots (cowboy ~) | сапоги (мн) | [sapa'gi] |
| slippers | тапочки (мн) | ['tapatʃki] |

tennis shoes (e.g., Nike ~)	кроссовки (мн)	[kra'sɔfki]
sneakers	кеды (мн)	['kedɪ]
(e.g., Converse ~)		
sandals	сандалии (мн)	[san'dali]

cobbler (shoe repairer)	сапожник (м)	[sa'poʒnik]
heel	каблук (м)	[kab'luk]
pair (of shoes)	пара (ж)	['parə]

| shoestring | шнурок (м) | [ʃnʊ'rɔk] |
| to lace (vt) | шнуровать | [ʃnʊra'vatʲ] |

| shoehorn | рожок (м) | [ra'ʒɔk] |
| shoe polish | крем (м) для обуви | [krem dʎa 'ɔbʊwi] |

37. Personal accessories

gloves	перчатки (ж мн)	[pir'tʃatki]
mittens	варежки (ж мн)	['variʃki]
scarf (muffler)	шарф (м)	[ʃʌrf]

glasses (eyeglasses)	очки (мн)	[atʃ'ki]
frame (eyeglass ~)	оправа (ж)	[ap'ravə]
umbrella	зонт (м)	[zont]
walking stick	трость (ж)	[trɔstʲ]

| hairbrush | щётка (ж) для волос | ['ɕatka dʎa va'lɔs] |
| fan | веер (м) | ['weer] |

| tie (necktie) | галстук (м) | ['galstʊk] |
| bow tie | галстук-бабочка (м) | [galstʊk 'babatʃkə] |

| suspenders | подтяжки (мн) | [pa'tʲaʃki] |
| handkerchief | носовой платок (м) | [nasa'vɔj pla'tɔk] |

| comb | расчёска (ж) | [ra'ɕaskə] |
| barrette | заколка (ж) | [za'kɔlkə] |

| hairpin | шпилька (ж) | [ʃʲpiʎkə] |
| buckle | пряжка (ж) | [pʲrʲaʃkə] |

| belt | пояс (м) | ['pɔis] |
| shoulder strap | ремень (м) | [ri'meɲ] |

bag (handbag)	сумка (ж)	['sʊmkə]
purse	сумочка (ж)	['sʊmatʃkə]
backpack	рюкзак (м)	[ryk'zak]

38. Clothing. Miscellaneous

fashion	мода (ж)	['mɔdə]
in vogue (adj)	модный	['mɔdnıj]
fashion designer	модельер (м)	[madɛ'ʎjer]

collar	воротник (м)	[varat'nik]
pocket	карман (м)	[kar'man]
pocket (as adj)	карманный	[kar'mannıj]
sleeve	рукав (м)	[rʊ'kaf]
hanging loop	вешалка (ж)	['weʃʌlkə]
fly (on trousers)	ширинка (ж)	[ʃı'rinkə]

zipper (fastener)	молния (ж)	['mɔlnija]
fastener	застёжка (ж)	[zas'tɜʃkə]
button	пуговица (ж)	['pʊgawitsə]
buttonhole	петля (ж)	[pit'ʎa]
to come off (ab. button)	оторваться	[atar'vatsə]

to sew (vi, vt)	шить	[ʃıtʲ]
to embroider (vi, vt)	вышивать	[vıʃı'vatʲ]
embroidery	вышивка (ж)	['vıʃıfkə]
sewing needle	иголка (ж)	[i'gɔlka]
thread	нитка (ж)	['nitkə]
seam	шов (м)	[ʃɔf]

to get dirty (vi)	испачкаться	[is'patʃkatsə]
stain (mark, spot)	пятно (с)	[pit'nɔ]
to crease, crumple (vi)	помяться	[pa'mʲatsə]
to tear, to rip (vt)	порвать	[par'vatʲ]
clothes moth	моль (м)	[mɔʎ]

39. Personal care. Cosmetics

toothpaste	зубная паста (ж)	[zub'naja 'pastə]
toothbrush	зубная щётка (ж)	[zub'naja 'ɕɔtkə]
to brush one's teeth	чистить зубы	['tʃistitʲ 'zubı]

razor	бритва (ж)	[b'ritvə]
shaving cream	крем (м) для бритья	[krem dʎa bri'tja]
to shave (vi)	бриться	[b'ritsə]

soap	мыло (с)	['mılə]
shampoo	шампунь (м)	[ʃʌm'pʊɲ]

scissors	ножницы (мн)	['nɔʒnitsı]
nail file	пилочка (ж) для ногтей	['pilatʃka dʎa nak'tej]
nail clippers	щипчики (мн)	['ɕiptʃiki]
tweezers	пинцет (м)	[pin'tsət]

cosmetics	косметика (ж)	[kas'metikə]
face mask	маска (ж)	['maskə]
manicure	маникюр (м)	[mani'kyr]
to have a manicure	делать маникюр	['delatʲ mani'kyr]
pedicure	педикюр (м)	[pidi'kyr]

make-up bag	косметичка (ж)	[kasme'titʃkə]
face powder	пудра (ж)	['pʊdrə]
powder compact	пудреница (ж)	['pʊdrinitsə]
blusher	румяна (ж)	[rʊ'mʲanə]

perfume (bottled)	духи (мн)	[dʊ'hi]
toilet water (perfume)	туалетная вода (ж)	[tʊɑ'letnaja va'da]
lotion	лосьон (м)	[la'sjon]
cologne	одеколон (м)	[adika'lɔn]

eyeshadow	тени (мн) для век	['teni dʎa 'wek]
eyeliner	карандаш (м) для глаз	[karan'daʃ dʎa g'las]
mascara	тушь (ж)	[tʊʃ]

lipstick	губная помада (ж)	[gʊb'naja pa'madə]
nail polish, enamel	лак (м) для ногтей	[lak dʎa nak'tej]
hair spray	лак (м) для волос	[lak dʎa va'lɔs]
deodorant	дезодорант (м)	[dizada'rant]

cream	крем (м)	[krem]
face cream	крем (м) для лица	[krem dʎa li'tsa]
hand cream	крем (м) для рук	[krem dʎa 'rʊk]
anti-wrinkle cream	крем (м) против морщин	[krem p'rotif mar'çin]
day cream	дневной крем (м)	[dniv'nɔj krem]
night cream	ночной крем (м)	[natʃ'nɔj krem]
day (as adj)	дневной	[dniv'nɔj]
night (as adj)	ночной	[natʃ'nɔj]

tampon	тампон (м)	[tam'pɔn]
toilet paper	туалетная бумага (ж)	[tʊɑ'letnaja bʊ'magə]
hair dryer	фен (м)	[fen]

40. Watches. Clocks

watch (wristwatch)	часы (мн)	[tʃi'sɪ]
dial	циферблат (м)	[tsɪferb'lat]
hand (of clock, watch)	стрелка (ж)	[st'relkə]
metal watch band	браслет (м)	[bras'let]
watch strap	ремешок (м)	[rime'ʃɔk]

battery	батарейка (ж)	[bata'rejkə]
to be dead (battery)	сесть	[sestʲ]
to change a battery	поменять батарейку	[pami'nʲatʲ bata'rejkʊ]
to run fast	спешить	[spi'ʃitʲ]

to run slow	отставать	[atsta'vatʲ]
wall clock	настенные часы (мн)	[nas'tennɪe tʃə'sɪ]
hourglass	песочные часы (мн)	[pe'sotʃnɪe tʃə'sɪ]
sundial	солнечные часы (мн)	['sɔlnitʃnɪe tʃi'sɪ]
alarm clock	будильник (м)	[bʊ'diʎnik]
watchmaker	часовщик (м)	[tʃisaʃ'ɕik]
to repair (vt)	ремонтировать	[riman'tiravatʲ]

T&P BOOKS

EVERYDAY EXPERIENCE

T&P Books Publishing

money	деньги (мн)	['deŋgi]
currency exchange	обмен (м)	[ab'men]
exchange rate	курс (м)	[kʊrs]
ATM	банкомат (м)	[banka'mat]
coin	монета (ж)	[ma'netə]

| dollar | доллар (м) | ['dɔllar] |
| euro | евро (с) | ['evrə] |

lira	лира (ж)	['lirə]
Deutschmark	марка (ж)	['markə]
franc	франк (м)	[frank]
pound sterling	фунт стерлингов (м)	[fʊnt s'terlihgaf]
yen	йена (ж)	['enə]

debt	долг (м)	[dɔlk]
debtor	должник (м)	[daʤ'nik]
to lend (money)	дать в долг	[datʲ v 'dɔlk]
to borrow (vi, vt)	взять в долг	[vzʲatʲ v 'dɔlk]

bank	банк (м)	[bank]
account	счёт (м)	['ɕ3t]
to deposit (vt)	положить	[pala'ʒitʲ]
to deposit into the account	положить на счёт	[pala'ʒitʲ na 'ɕ3t]
to withdraw (vt)	снять со счёта	[s'natʲ sa 'ɕ3tə]

credit card	кредитная карта (ж)	[kri'ditnaja 'kartə]
cash	наличные деньги (мн)	[na'liʧnɪe 'deŋgi]
check	чек (м)	[ʧek]
to write a check	выписать чек	['vɪpisatʲ ʧek]
checkbook	чековая книжка (ж)	['ʧekavaja k'niʃkə]

wallet	бумажник (м)	[bʊ'maʒnik]
change purse	кошелёк (м)	[kaʃi'lɜk]
billfold	портмоне (с)	[partma'nɛ]
safe	сейф (м)	[sɛjf]

heir	наследник (м)	[nas'lednik]
inheritance	наследство (с)	[nas'letstvə]
fortune (wealth)	состояние (с)	[sasta'janie]

lease	аренда (ж)	[a'rendə]
rent (money)	квартирная плата (ж)	[kvar'tirnaja p'latə]
to rent (sth from sb)	снимать	[sni'matʲ]

price	цена (ж)	[tsɪ'na]
cost	стоимость (ж)	[s'tɔimastʲ]
sum	сумма (ж)	['sʊmmə]

to spend (vt)	тратить	[tra'titʲ]
expenses	расходы (мн)	[ras'hɔdɪ]
to economize (vi, vt)	экономить	[ɛka'nɔmitʲ]
economical	экономный	[ɛka'nɔmnɪj]

to pay (vi, vt)	платить	[pla'titʲ]
payment	оплата (ж)	[ap'latə]
change (give the ~)	сдача (ж)	[z'datʃə]

tax	налог (м)	[na'lɔk]
fine	штраф (м)	[ʃtraf]
to fine (vt)	штрафовать	[ʃtrafa'vatʲ]

42. Post. Postal service

post office	почта (ж)	['pɔtʃtə]
mail (letters, etc.)	почта (ж)	['pɔtʃtə]
mailman	почтальон (м)	[patʃta'ʎjon]
opening hours	часы (мн) работы	[tʃa'sɪ ra'bɔtɪ]

letter	письмо (с)	[pisʲ'mɔ]
registered letter	заказное письмо (с)	[zakaz'nɔe pisʲ'mɔ]
postcard	открытка (ж)	[atk'rɪtkə]
telegram	телеграмма (ж)	[tileg'ramə]
package (parcel)	посылка (ж)	[pa'sɪlkə]
money transfer	денежный перевод (м)	['deneʒnɪj piri'vɔt]

to receive (vt)	получить	[palu'tʃitʲ]
to send (vt)	отправить	[atp'rawitʲ]
sending	отправка (ж)	[atp'rafkə]

address	адрес (м)	['adres]
ZIP code	индекс (м)	['indɛks]
sender	отправитель (м)	[atpra'witeʎ]
receiver	получатель (м)	[palu'tʃateʎ]

| name (first name) | имя (с) | ['imʲa] |
| surname (last name) | фамилия (ж) | [fa'milija] |

postage rate	тариф (м)	[ta'rif]
standard (adj)	обычный	[a'bɪtʃnɪj]
economical (adj)	экономичный	[ikana'mitʃnɪj]

weight	вес (м)	[wes]
to weigh (~ letters)	взвешивать	[vz'weʃivatʲ]
envelope	конверт (м)	[kan'wert]

| postage stamp | марка (ж) | ['markə] |
| to stamp an envelope | наклеивать марку | [nak'leivatʲ 'markʊ] |

43. Banking

| bank | банк (м) | [bank] |
| branch (of bank, etc.) | отделение (с) | [addi'lenie] |

| bank clerk, consultant | консультант (м) | [kansʊˈtant] |
| manager (director) | управляющий (м) | [uprav'ʌajuɕij] |

bank account	счёт (м)	[ˈɕɜt]
account number	номер (м) счёта	['nɔmer 'ɕɜtə]
checking account	текущий счёт (м)	[te'kʊɕij 'ɕɜt]
savings account	накопительный счёт (м)	[naka'piteʌnij 'ɕɜt]

to open an account	открыть счёт	[atkrɨtʲ 'ɕɜt]
to close the account	закрыть счёт	[zak'rɨtʲ 'ɕɜt]
to deposit into the account	положить на счёт	[pala'ʒitʲ na 'ɕɜt]
to withdraw (vt)	снять со счёта	[s'natʲ sa 'ɕɜtə]

| deposit | вклад (м) | [vklat] |
| to make a deposit | сделать вклад | [z'delatʲ fklat] |

| wire transfer | перевод (м) | [pere'vɔt] |
| to wire, to transfer | сделать перевод | [z'delatʲ pere'vɔt] |

| sum | сумма (ж) | ['sʊmmə] |
| How much? | Сколько? | [s'kɔʌka] |

| signature | подпись (ж) | ['pɔtpisʲ] |
| to sign (vt) | подписать | [patpi'satʲ] |

| credit card | кредитная карта (ж) | [kri'ditnaja 'kartə] |
| code (PIN code) | код (м) | [kɔt] |

| credit card number | номер (м) кредитной карты | ['nɔmer kre'ditnaj 'kartɪ] |

| ATM | банкомат (м) | [banka'mat] |

check	чек (м)	[tʃek]
to write a check	выписать чек	['vɨpisatʲ tʃek]
checkbook	чековая книжка (ж)	['tʃekavaja k'niʃkə]

| loan (bank ~) | кредит (м) | [kri'dit] |
| to apply for a loan | обращаться за кредитом | [abra'ɕatsa za kre'ditam] |

to get a loan	брать кредит	[bratʲ kre'dit]
to give a loan	предоставлять кредит	[pridastav'ʌatʲ kri'dit]
guarantee	гарантия (ж)	[ga'rantija]

44. Telephone. Phone conversation

telephone	телефон (м)	[tɪle'fɔn]
mobile phone	мобильный телефон (м)	[ma'biʎnɪj tele'fɔn]
answering machine	автоответчик (м)	[aftaat'wetʃik]
to call (by phone)	звонить	[zva'nɪtʲ]
phone call	звонок (м)	[zva'nɔk]
to dial a number	набрать номер	[nab'ratʲ 'nɔmer]
Hello!	Алло!	[a'lɔ]
to ask (vt)	спросить	[spra'sitʲ]
to answer (vi, vt)	ответить	[at'wetitʲ]
to hear (vt)	слышать	[s'lɪʃtʲ]
well (adv)	хорошо	[hara'ʃɔ]
not well (adv)	плохо	[p'lɔhə]
noises (interference)	помехи (ж мн)	[pa'mehi]
receiver	трубка (ж)	[t'rupkə]
to pick up (~ the phone)	снять трубку	[sɲatʲ t'rupkʊ]
to hang up (~ the phone)	положить трубку	[pala'ʒitʲ t'rupkʊ]
busy (adj)	занятый	['zanitɪj]
to ring (ab. phone)	звонить	[zva'nɪtʲ]
telephone book	телефонная книга (ж)	[tele'fɔnnaja k'nigə]
local (adj)	местный	['mesnɪj]
local call	местный звонок (м)	['mesnɪj zva'nɔk]
long distance (~ call)	междугородний	[miʒdʊga'rɔdnɪj]
long-distance call	междугородний звонок (м)	[miʒdʊga'rɔdnɪj zva'nɔk]
international (adj)	международный	[miʒdʊna'rɔdnɪj]
international call	международный звонок	[miʒdʊna'rɔdnɪj zva'nɔk]

45. Mobile telephone

mobile phone	мобильный телефон (м)	[ma'biʎnɪj tele'fɔn]
display	дисплей (м)	[disp'lej]
button	кнопка (ж)	[k'nɔpkə]
SIM card	SIM-карта (ж)	[sim 'kartə]
battery	батарея (ж)	[bata'reja]
to be dead (battery)	разрядиться	[razri'ditsə]
charger	зарядное устройство (с)	[za'rʲadnae ust'rɔjstvə]
menu	меню (с)	[mi'ny]
settings	настройки (ж мн)	[nast'rɔjki]

| tune (melody) | мелодия (ж) | [mi'lɔdija] |
| to select (vt) | выбрать | ['vɪbratʲ] |

calculator	калькулятор (м)	[kaʎkʊ'ʎatar]
voice mail	автоответчик (м)	[aftaat'wetʃik]
alarm clock	будильник (м)	[bʊ'diʎnik]
contacts	телефонная книга (ж)	[tele'fɔnnaja kʲnigə]

| SMS (text message) | SMS-сообщение (с) | [ɛsɛ'mɛs saap'ɕenie] |
| subscriber | абонент (м) | [aba'nent] |

46. Stationery

| ballpoint pen | шариковая ручка | ['ʃʌrikɔvaja 'rʊtʃka] |
| fountain pen | перьевая ручка | [pirje'vaja 'rʊtʃka] |

pencil	карандаш (м)	[karan'daʃ]
highlighter	маркер (м)	['marker]
felt-tip pen	фломастер (м)	[fla'master]

| notepad | блокнот (м) | [blak'nɔt] |
| agenda (diary) | ежедневник (м) | [eʒɪd'nevnik] |

ruler	линейка (ж)	[li'nejkə]
calculator	калькулятор (м)	[kaʎkʊ'ʎatar]
eraser	ластик (м)	['lastik]
thumbtack	кнопка (ж)	[k'nɔpkə]
paper clip	скрепка (ж)	[sk'repkə]

glue	клей (м)	[klej]
stapler	степлер (м)	[s'tepler]
hole punch	дырокол (м)	[dɪra'kɔl]
pencil sharpener	точилка (ж)	[ta'tʃilkə]

47. Foreign languages

language	язык (м)	[ja'zɪk]
foreign (adj)	иностранный	[inast'rannɪj]
foreign language	иностранный язык (м)	[inast'rannɪj ja'zɪk]
to study (vt)	изучать	[izu'tʃatʲ]
to learn (language, etc.)	учить	[u'tʃitʲ]

to read (vi, vt)	читать	[tʃi'tatʲ]
to speak (vi, vt)	говорить	[gava'ritʲ]
to understand (vt)	понимать	[pani'matʲ]
to write (vt)	писать	[pi'satʲ]
fast (adv)	быстро	['bɪstrə]
slowly (adv)	медленно	['medlenə]

fluently (adv)	свободно	[sva'bɔdnə]
rules	правила (с мн)	[p'rawilə]
grammar	грамматика (ж)	[gra'mɑtikə]
vocabulary	лексика (ж)	['lɛksikə]
phonetics	фонетика (ж)	[fa'nɛtikə]

textbook	учебник (м)	[u'tʃebnik]
dictionary	словарь (м)	[sla'varʲ]
teach-yourself book	самоучитель (м)	[samau'tʃiteʎ]
phrasebook	разговорник (м)	[razga'vɔrnik]

cassette	кассета (ж)	[ka'setə]
videotape	видеокассета (ж)	[wideaka'setə]
CD, compact disc	компакт диск (м)	[kam'pakt disk]
DVD	DVD-диск (м)	[diwi'di 'disk]

alphabet	алфавит (м)	[alfa'wit]
to spell (vt)	говорить по буквам	[gava'ritʲ pa 'bʊkvam]
pronunciation	произношение (с)	[praizna'ʃɛnie]

accent	акцент (м)	[ak'tsɛnt]
with an accent	с акцентом	[s ak'tsɛntam]
without an accent	без акцента	[bez ak'tsɛntə]

| word | слово (с) | [s'lɔvə] |
| meaning | смысл (м) | [smɪsl] |

course (e.g., a French ~)	курсы (мн)	['kʊrsɪ]
to sign up	записаться	[zapi'satsə]
teacher	преподаватель (м)	[pripada'vateʎ]

translation (process)	перевод (м)	[pere'vɔt]
translation (text, etc.)	перевод (м)	[pere'vɔt]
translator	переводчик (м)	[pire'vɔtʃik]
interpreter	переводчик (м)	[pire'vɔtʃik]

| polyglot | полиглот (м) | [palig'lɔt] |
| memory | память (ж) | ['pamitʲ] |

T&P BOOKS

MEALS. RESTAURANT

T&P Books Publishing

48. Table setting

spoon	ложка (ж)	['lɔʃkə]
knife	нож (м)	[nɔʃ]
fork	вилка (ж)	['wilkə]
cup (e.g., coffee ~)	чашка (ж)	['ʧaʃkə]
plate (dinner ~)	тарелка (ж)	[tɑ'relkə]
saucer	блюдце (с)	[b'lyʦe]
napkin (on table)	салфетка (ж)	[sal'fetkə]
toothpick	зубочистка (ж)	[zubɑ'ʧistkə]

49. Restaurant

restaurant	ресторан (м)	[ristɑ'ran]
coffee house	кофейня (ж)	[ka'fejɲa]
pub, bar	бар (м)	[bar]
tearoom	чайный салон (м)	['ʧajnɪj sɑ'lɔn]
waiter	официант (м)	[afɪtsɪ'ant]
waitress	официантка (ж)	[afɪtsɪ'antkə]
bartender	бармен (м)	[bar'men]
menu	меню (с)	[mi'ny]
wine list	карта (ж) вин	['karta win]
to book a table	забронировать столик	[zabrɑ'niravatʲ s'tɔlik]
course, dish	блюдо (с)	[b'lydə]
to order (meal)	заказать	[zaka'zatʲ]
to make an order	сделать заказ	[s'delatʲ za'kas]
aperitif	аперитив (м)	[apiri'tif]
appetizer	закуска (ж)	[za'kʊskə]
dessert	десерт (м)	[di'sert]
check	счёт (м)	['ɕɔt]
to pay the check	оплатить счёт	[apla'titʲ 'ɕɔt]
to give change	дать сдачу	[datʲ s'datʃu]
tip	чаевые (мн)	[ʧii'vɪe]

50. Meals

food	еда (ж)	[e'da]
to eat (vi, vt)	есть	[estʲ]

breakfast	завтрак (м)	['zaftrak]
to have breakfast	завтракать	['zaftrakatʲ]
lunch	обед (м)	[a'bet]
to have lunch	обедать	[a'bedatʲ]
dinner	ужин (м)	['uʒɪn]
to have dinner	ужинать	['uʒɪnatʲ]

| appetite | аппетит (м) | [api'tit] |
| Enjoy your meal! | Приятного аппетита! | [pri'jatnava ape'tita] |

to open (~ a bottle)	открывать	[atkrɪ'vatʲ]
to spill (liquid)	пролить	[pra'litʲ]
to spill out (vi)	пролиться	[pra'litsə]

to boil (vi)	кипеть	[ki'petʲ]
to boil (vt)	кипятить	[kipi'titʲ]
boiled (~ water)	кипячёный	[kipi'tʃonɪj]
to chill, cool down (vt)	охладить	[ahla'ditʲ]
to chill (vi)	охлаждаться	[ahlaʒ'datsə]

| taste, flavor | вкус (м) | [fkʊs] |
| aftertaste | привкус (м) | [p'rifkʊs] |

to slim down (lose weight)	худеть	[hʊ'detʲ]
diet	диета (ж)	[di'etə]
vitamin	витамин (м)	[wita'min]
calorie	калория (ж)	[ka'lɔrija]
vegetarian (n)	вегетарианец (м)	[wigitari'anets]
vegetarian (adj)	вегетарианский	[wigitari'anskij]

fats (nutrient)	жиры (мн)	[ʒɪ'rɪ]
proteins	белки (мн)	[bil'ki]
carbohydrates	углеводы (мн)	[ugle'vɔdɪ]
slice (of lemon, ham)	ломтик (м)	['lomtik]
piece (of cake, pie)	кусок (м)	[kʊ'sɔk]
crumb (of bread, cake, etc.)	крошка (ж)	[k'rɔʃkə]

51. Cooked dishes

course, dish	блюдо (с)	[b'lydə]
cuisine	кухня (ж)	['kʊhɲa]
recipe	рецепт (м)	[ri'tsəpt]
portion	порция (ж)	['pɔrtsija]

| salad | салат (м) | [sa'lat] |
| soup | суп (м) | [sʊp] |

| clear soup (broth) | бульон (м) | [bʊ'ʎjon] |
| sandwich (bread) | бутерброд (м) | [bʊterb'rɔt] |

fried eggs	яичница (ж)	[i'iʃnitsə]
fried meatballs	котлета (ж)	[kat'letə]
hamburger (beefburger)	гамбургер (м)	['gamburger]
beefsteak	бифштекс (м)	[bifʃ'tɛks]
stew	жаркое (с)	[ʒar'kɔe]

side dish	гарнир (м)	[gar'nir]
spaghetti	спагетти (мн)	[spa'getti]
mashed potatoes	картофельное пюре (с)	[kar'tɔfeʌnae py'rɛ]
pizza	пицца (ж)	['pitsə]
porridge (oatmeal, etc.)	каша (ж)	['kaʃə]
omelet	омлет (м)	[am'let]

boiled (e.g., ~ beef)	варёный	[va'rɜnɪj]
smoked (adj)	копчёный	[kap'tʃɔnɪj]
fried (adj)	жареный	['ʒarenɪj]
dried (adj)	сушёный	[su'ʃɔnɪj]
frozen (adj)	замороженный	[zama'rɔʒɪnɪj]
pickled (adj)	маринованный	[mari'nɔvanɪj]

sweet (sugary)	сладкий	[s'latkij]
salty (adj)	солёный	[sa'lɜnɪj]
cold (adj)	холодный	[ha'lɔdnɪj]
hot (adj)	горячий	[ga'rʲatʃij]
bitter (adj)	горький	['gɔrʲkij]
tasty (adj)	вкусный	[f'kusnɪj]

to cook in boiling water	варить	[va'ritʲ]
to cook (dinner)	готовить	[ga'tɔwitʲ]
to fry (vt)	жарить	['ʒaritʲ]
to heat up (food)	разогревать	[razagre'vatʲ]

to salt (vt)	солить	[sa'litʲ]
to pepper (vt)	перчить	[pir'tʃitʲ]
to grate (vt)	тереть	[ti'retʲ]
peel (n)	кожура (ж)	[kaʒu'ra]
to peel (vt)	чистить	['tʃistitʲ]

52. Food

meat	мясо (с)	['mʲasə]
chicken	курица (ж)	['kuritsə]
Rock Cornish hen (poussin)	цыплёнок (м)	[tsɪp'lɜnak]
duck	утка (ж)	['utkə]
goose	гусь (м)	[gusʲ]
game	дичь (ж)	[ditʃ]
turkey	индейка (ж)	[in'dejkə]
pork	свинина (ж)	[swi'ninə]
veal	телятина (ж)	[ti'ʌatinə]

lamb	баранина (ж)	[bɑ'rɑninə]
beef	говядина (ж)	[gɑ'vʲadinə]
rabbit	кролик (м)	[k'rɔlik]

sausage (bologna, pepperoni, etc.)	колбаса (ж)	[kɑlbɑ'sɑ]
vienna sausage (frankfurter)	сосиска (ж)	[sɑ'siskə]
bacon	бекон (м)	[bi'kɔn]
ham	ветчина (ж)	[witʃi'nɑ]
gammon	окорок (м)	['ɔkɑrɑk]

pâté	паштет (м)	[pɑʃ'tet]
liver	печень (ж)	['petʃeɲ]
lard	сало (с)	['salə]
hamburger (ground beef)	фарш (м)	[fɑrʃ]
tongue	язык (м)	[ja'zɨk]

egg	яйцо (с)	[jaj'tsɔ]
eggs	яйца (мн)	['jajtsə]
egg white	белок (м)	[bi'lɔk]
egg yolk	желток (м)	[ʒɨl'tɔk]

fish	рыба (ж)	['rɨbə]
seafood	морепродукты (мн)	[mɑreprɑ'dʊktɨ]
crustaceans	ракообразные (мн)	[rakaɑb'raznɪe]
caviar	икра (ж)	[ik'ra]

crab	краб (м)	[krɑp]
shrimp	креветка (ж)	[kri'wetkə]
oyster	устрица (ж)	['ustritsə]
spiny lobster	лангуст (м)	[lɑ'ŋust]
octopus	осьминог (м)	[asʲmi'nɔk]
squid	кальмар (м)	[kɑʎ'mɑr]

sturgeon	осетрина (ж)	[asit'rinə]
salmon	лосось (м)	[lɑ'sɔsʲ]
halibut	палтус (м)	['pɑltʊs]

cod	треска (ж)	[tris'kɑ]
mackerel	скумбрия (ж)	[s'kumbrija]
tuna	тунец (м)	[tʊ'nets]
eel	угорь (м)	['ugɑrʲ]

trout	форель (ж)	[fɑ'reʎ]
sardine	сардина (ж)	[sɑr'dinə]
pike	щука (ж)	['ɕukə]
herring	сельдь (ж)	[seʎtʲ]

bread	хлеб (м)	[hlep]
cheese	сыр (м)	[sɨr]
sugar	сахар (м)	['sahɑr]

salt	соль (ж)	[sɔʎ]
rice	рис (м)	[ris]
pasta	макароны (мн)	[maka'rɔnɪ]
noodles	лапша (ж)	[lap'ʃʌ]

butter	сливочное масло (с)	[s'livatʃnae 'maslə]
vegetable oil	растительное масло (с)	[ras'titeʎnae 'maslə]
sunflower oil	подсолнечное масло (с)	[pa'tsɔlnetʃnae 'maslə]
margarine	маргарин (м)	[marga'rin]

| olives | оливки (мн) | [a'lifki] |
| olive oil | оливковое масло (с) | [a'lifkavae 'maslə] |

milk	молоко (с)	[mala'kɔ]
condensed milk	сгущённое молоко (с)	[sgʊ'ɕɜnae mala'kɔ]
yogurt	йогурт (м)	['jogʊrt]
sour cream	сметана (ж)	[smi'tanə]
cream (of milk)	сливки (мн)	[s'lifki]

| mayonnaise | майонез (м) | [mai'nɛs] |
| buttercream | крем (м) | [krem] |

cereal grains (wheat, etc.)	крупа (ж)	[krʊ'pa]
flour	мука (ж)	[mʊ'ka]
canned food	консервы (мн)	[kan'servɪ]

cornflakes	кукурузные хлопья (мн)	[kʊkʊ'rʊznɪe h'lɔpja]
honey	мёд (м)	['mɜt]
jam	джем, конфитюр	[dʒɛm], [kanfi'tyr]
chewing gum	жевательная резинка (м)	[ʒɪ'vateʎnaja re'zinkə]

53. Drinks

water	вода (ж)	[va'da]
drinking water	питьевая вода (ж)	[pitje'vaja va'da]
mineral water	минеральная вода (ж)	[mini'raʎnaja va'da]

still (adj)	без газа	[bez 'gazə]
carbonated (adj)	газированная	[gazi'rɔvanaja]
sparkling (adj)	с газом	[s gazam]
ice	лёд (м)	['lɜt]
with ice	со льдом	[saʎ'dɔm]

non-alcoholic (adj)	безалкогольный	[bizalka'gɔʎnɪj]
soft drink	безалкогольный напиток (м)	[bizalka'gɔʎnɪj na'pitak]
refreshing drink	прохладительный напиток (м)	[prahla'diteʎnɪj na'pitak]
lemonade	лимонад (м)	[lima'nat]

liquors	алкогольные напитки (мн)	[alka'gɔʎnɪe na'pitki]
wine	вино (с)	[wi'nɔ]
white wine	белое вино (с)	['belae wi'nɔ]
red wine	красное вино (с)	[k'rasnae wi'nɔ]

liqueur	ликёр (м)	[li'kɜr]
champagne	шампанское (с)	[ʃʌm'panskae]
vermouth	вермут (м)	['wermʊt]

whisky	виски (с)	['wiski]
vodka	водка (ж)	['vɔtkə]
gin	джин (м)	[dʒɪn]
cognac	коньяк (м)	[ka'njak]
rum	ром (м)	[rɔm]

coffee	кофе (м)	['kɔfe]
black coffee	чёрный кофе (м)	['tʃɔrnɪj 'kɔfe]
coffee with milk	кофе (м) с молоком	['kɔfe s mala'kɔm]
cappuccino	кофе (м) со сливками	['kɔfe sa s'lifkami]
instant coffee	растворимый кофе (м)	[rastva'rimɪj 'kɔfe]

milk	молоко (с)	[mala'kɔ]
cocktail	коктейль (м)	[kak'tɛjʎ]
milkshake	молочный коктейль (м)	[ma'lɔtʃnɪj kak'tɛjʎ]

juice	сок (м)	[sɔk]
tomato juice	томатный сок (м)	[ta'matnɪj sɔk]
orange juice	апельсиновый сок (м)	[apiʎ'sinavɪj sɔk]
freshly squeezed juice	свежевыжатый сок (м)	[sweʒɛ'vɪʒatɪj sɔk]

beer	пиво (с)	['pivə]
light beer	светлое пиво (с)	[s'wetlae 'pivə]
dark beer	тёмное пиво (с)	['tɜmnae 'pivə]

tea	чай (м)	[tʃaj]
black tea	чёрный чай (м)	['tʃɔrnɪj tʃaj]
green tea	зелёный чай (м)	[zi'lɜnɪj tʃaj]

54. Vegetables

| vegetables | овощи (м мн) | ['ɔvaɕi] |
| greens | зелень (ж) | ['zeleɲ] |

tomato	помидор (м)	[pami'dɔr]
cucumber	огурец (м)	[agʊ'rets]
carrot	морковь (ж)	[mar'kɔfʲ]
potato	картофель (м)	[kar'tɔfeʎ]
onion	лук (м)	[luk]
garlic	чеснок (м)	[tʃis'nɔk]

cabbage	капуста (ж)	[ka'pustə]
cauliflower	цветная капуста (ж)	[tswet'naja ka'pustə]
Brussels sprouts	брюссельская капуста (ж)	[bry'seʌskaja ka'pustə]
broccoli	капуста брокколи (ж)	[ka'pusta b'rɔkali]
beetroot	свёкла (ж)	['swɜklə]
eggplant	баклажан (м)	[bakla'ʒan]
zucchini	кабачок (м)	[kaba'tʃok]
pumpkin	тыква (ж)	['tɪkvə]
turnip	репа (ж)	['repə]
parsley	петрушка (ж)	[pit'ruʃkə]
dill	укроп (м)	[uk'rɔp]
lettuce	салат (м)	[sa'lat]
celery	сельдерей (м)	[siʌde'rej]
asparagus	спаржа (ж)	[s'parʒə]
spinach	шпинат (м)	[ʃpi'nat]
pea	горох (м)	[ga'rɔh]
beans	бобы (мн)	[ba'bɪ]
corn (maize)	кукуруза (ж)	[kuku'ruzə]
kidney bean	фасоль (ж)	[fa'sɔʌ]
bell pepper	перец (м)	['perets]
radish	редис (м)	[ri'dis]
artichoke	артишок (м)	[arti'ʃɔk]

55. Fruits. Nuts

fruit	фрукт (м)	[frukt]
apple	яблоко (с)	['jablakə]
pear	груша (ж)	[g'ruʃə]
lemon	лимон (м)	[li'mɔn]
orange	апельсин (м)	[apiʌ'sin]
strawberry	клубника (ж)	[klub'nikə]
mandarin	мандарин (м)	[manda'rin]
plum	слива (ж)	[s'livə]
peach	персик (м)	['persik]
apricot	абрикос (м)	[abri'kɔs]
raspberry	малина (ж)	[ma'linə]
pineapple	ананас (м)	[ana'nas]
banana	банан (м)	[ba'nan]
watermelon	арбуз (м)	[ar'bus]
grape	виноград (м)	[winag'rat]
sour cherry	вишня (ж)	['wiʃna]
sweet cherry	черешня (ж)	[tʃi'reʃna]
melon	дыня (ж)	['dɪnə]

grapefruit	грейпфрут (м)	[gripf'rʊt]
avocado	авокадо (с)	[ava'kadə]
papaya	папайя (ж)	[pa'paja]
mango	манго (с)	['mɑhgə]
pomegranate	гранат (м)	[gra'nɑt]

redcurrant	красная смородина (ж)	[k'rasnaja sma'rɔdinə]
blackcurrant	чёрная смородина (ж)	['ʧɔrnaja sma'rɔdinə]
gooseberry	крыжовник (м)	[krɪ'ʒɔvnik]
bilberry	черника (ж)	[ʧir'nikə]
blackberry	ежевика (ж)	[eʒɪ'wikə]

raisin	изюм (м)	[i'zym]
fig	инжир (м)	[in'ʒir]
date	финик (м)	['finik]

peanut	арахис (м)	[a'rɑhis]
almond	миндаль (м)	[min'daʎ]
walnut	грецкий орех (м)	[g'retskij a'reh]
hazelnut	лесной орех (м)	[lis'nɔj a'reh]
coconut	кокосовый орех (м)	[ka'kɔsavɪj a'reh]
pistachios	фисташки (мн)	[fis'taʃki]

56. Bread. Candy

bakers' confectionery (pastry)	кондитерские изделия (мн)	[kan'diterskie iz'delija]
bread	хлеб (м)	[hlep]
cookies	печенье (с)	[pi'ʧeɲje]

chocolate (n)	шоколад (м)	[ʃʌka'lat]
chocolate (as adj)	шоколадный	[ʃʌka'ladnɪj]
candy	конфета (ж)	[kan'fetə]
cake (e.g., cupcake)	пирожное (с)	[pi'rɔʒnae]
cake (e.g., birthday ~)	торт (м)	[tɔrt]
pie (e.g., apple ~)	пирог (м)	[pi'rɔk]
filling (for cake, pie)	начинка (ж)	[na'ʧinkə]

whole fruit jam	варенье (с)	[va'reɲje]
marmalade	мармелад (м)	[marme'lat]
waffles	вафли (мн)	['vafli]
ice-cream	мороженое (с)	[ma'rɔʒnae]
pudding	пудинг (м)	['pʊdink]

57. Spices

| salt | соль (ж) | [sɔʎ] |
| salty (adj) | солёный | [sa'lɜnɪj] |

to salt (л)	солить	[sɑ'litʲ]
black pepper	чёрный перец (м)	['tʃɔrnɪj 'perets]
red pepper (milled ~)	красный перец (м)	[k'rɑsnɪj 'perets]
mustard	горчица (ж)	[gɑr'tʃitsə]
horseradish	хрен (м)	[hren]
condiment	приправа (ж)	[prip'rɑvə]
spice	пряность (ж)	[p'rʲanɑstʲ]
sauce	соус (м)	['sɔus]
vinegar	уксус (м)	['uksus]
anise	анис (м)	[ɑ'nis]
basil	базилик (м)	[bɑzi'lik]
cloves	гвоздика (ж)	[gvɑz'dikə]
ginger	имбирь (м)	[im'birʲ]
coriander	кориандр (м)	[kɑri'ɑndr]
cinnamon	корица (ж)	[kɑ'ritsə]
sesame	кунжут (м)	[kʊn'ʒut]
bay leaf	лавровый лист (м)	[lɑv'rɔvɪj list]
paprika	паприка (ж)	['pɑprikə]
caraway	тмин (м)	[tmin]
saffron	шафран (м)	[ʃʌf'rɑn]

PERSONAL INFORMATION. FAMILY

T&P Books Publishing

58. Personal information. Forms

name (first name)	имя (с)	['imʲa]
surname (last name)	фамилия (ж)	[fa'milija]
date of birth	дата (ж) рождения	['data raʒ'denija]
place of birth	место (с) рождения	['mesta raʒ'denija]
nationality	национальность (ж)	[natsɪɑ'naʎnastʲ]
place of residence	место (с) жительства	['mesta 'ʒiteʎstvə]
country	страна (ж)	[stra'na]
profession (occupation)	профессия (ж)	[pra'fesija]
gender, sex	пол (м)	[pɔl]
height	рост (м)	[rɔst]
weight	вес (м)	[wes]

59. Family members. Relatives

mother	мать (ж)	[matʲ]
father	отец (м)	[a'tets]
son	сын (м)	[sɪn]
daughter	дочь (ж)	[dɔtʃ]
younger daughter	младшая дочь (ж)	[m'latʃʌja dɔtʃ]
younger son	младший сын (м)	[m'latʃij sɪn]
eldest daughter	старшая дочь (ж)	[s'tarʃʌja dɔtʃ]
eldest son	старший сын (м)	[s'tarʃij sɪn]
brother	брат (м)	[brat]
sister	сестра (ж)	[sist'ra]
cousin (masc.)	двоюродный брат (м)	[dva'juradnɪj brat]
cousin (fem.)	двоюродная сестра (ж)	[dva'juradnaja sist'ra]
mom, mommy	мама (ж)	['mamə]
dad, daddy	папа (м)	['papə]
parents	родители (мн)	[ra'diteli]
child	ребёнок (м)	[ri'bɜnak]
children	дети (мн)	['deti]
grandmother	бабушка (ж)	['babʊʃkə]
grandfather	дедушка (м)	['dedʊʃkə]
grandson	внук (м)	[vnʊk]
granddaughter	внучка (ж)	[v'nʊtʃkə]
grandchildren	внуки (мн)	[v'nʊki]

uncle	дядя (м)	['dʲadʲa]
aunt	тётя (ж)	['tɜtʲa]
nephew	племянник (м)	[pli'mʲanik]
niece	племянница (ж)	[pli'mʲanitsə]

mother-in-law (wife's mother)	тёща (ж)	['tɜɕə]
father-in-law (husband's father)	свёкор (м)	['swɜkɑr]
son-in-law (daughter's husband)	зять (м)	[zʲatʲ]
stepmother	мачеха (ж)	['matʃehə]
stepfather	отчим (м)	['ɔtʃim]

infant	грудной ребенок (м)	[grʊd'nɔj ri'bɜnɑk]
baby (infant)	младенец (м)	[mla'denets]
little boy, kid	малыш (м)	[ma'lɪʃ]

wife	жена (ж)	[ʒɪ'na]
husband	муж (м)	[mʊʃ]
spouse (husband)	супруг (м)	[sʊp'rʊk]
spouse (wife)	супруга (ж)	[sʊp'rʊgə]

married (masc.)	женатый	[ʒɪ'natɪj]
married (fem.)	замужняя	[za'mʊʒnija]
single (unmarried)	холостой	[halas'tɔj]
bachelor	холостяк (м)	[halas'tʲak]
divorced (masc.)	разведённый	[razwe'dɜnɪj]
widow	вдова (ж)	[vda'va]
widower	вдовец (м)	[vda'wets]

relative	родственник (м)	['rɔtstwenik]
close relative	близкий родственник (м)	[b'liskij 'rɔtstwenik]
distant relative	дальний родственник (м)	['daʎnij 'rɔtstwenik]
relatives	родные (мн)	[rad'nɪe]

orphan (boy)	сирота (м)	[sira'ta]
orphan (girl)	сирота (ж)	[sira'ta]
guardian (of minor)	опекун (м)	[api'kʊn]
to adopt (a boy)	усыновить	[usɪna'witʲ]
to adopt (a girl)	удочерить	[udatʃe'ritʲ]

60. Friends. Coworkers

friend (masc.)	друг (м)	[drʊk]
friend (fem.)	подруга (ж)	[pad'rʊgə]
friendship	дружба (ж)	[d'rʊʒbə]
to be friends	дружить	[drʊ'ʒitʲ]

buddy (masc.)	приятель (м)	[pri'jateʎ]
buddy (fem.)	приятельница (ж)	[pri'jateʎnitsə]
partner	партнёр (м)	[part'nɜr]

chief (boss)	шеф (м)	[ʃəf]
superior (n)	начальник (м)	[na'tʃaʎnik]
owner, proprietor	владелец (м)	[vla'delets]
subordinate (n)	подчинённый (м)	[patʃi'nɜnnɪj]
colleague	коллега (м)	[ka'legə]

acquaintance (person)	знакомый (м)	[zna'kɔmɪj]
fellow traveler	попутчик (м)	[pa'putʃik]
classmate	одноклассник (м)	[adnak'lasnik]

neighbor (masc.)	сосед (м)	[sa'set]
neighbor (fem.)	соседка (ж)	[sa'setkə]
neighbors	соседи (мн)	[sa'sedi]

T&P BOOKS

HUMAN BODY. MEDICINE

T&P Books Publishing

head	голова (ж)	[gala'va]
face	лицо (с)	[li'tsɔ]
nose	нос (м)	[nɔs]
mouth	рот (м)	[rɔt]
eye	глаз (м)	[glas]
eyes	глаза (мн)	[gla'za]
pupil	зрачок (м)	[zra'tʃɔk]
eyebrow	бровь (ж)	[brɔfʲ]
eyelash	ресница (ж)	[ris'nitsə]
eyelid	веко (с)	['wekə]
tongue	язык (м)	[ja'zık]
tooth	зуб (м)	[zup]
lips	губы (мн)	['gʊbı]
cheekbones	скулы (мн)	[s'kʊlı]
gum	десна (ж)	[dis'na]
palate	нёбо (с)	['nɔbə]
nostrils	ноздри (мн)	['nɔzdri]
chin	подбородок (м)	[padba'rɔdak]
jaw	челюсть (ж)	['tʃelystʲ]
cheek	щека (ж)	[ɕi'ka]
forehead	лоб (м)	[lɔp]
temple	висок (м)	[wi'sɔk]
ear	ухо (с)	['uhə]
back of the head	затылок (м)	[za'tılak]
neck	шея (ж)	[ʃəja]
throat	горло (с)	['gɔrlə]
hair	волосы (мн)	['vɔlası]
hairstyle	причёска (ж)	[pri'tʃɔskə]
haircut	стрижка (ж)	[st'riʃkə]
wig	парик (м)	[pa'rik]
mustache	усы (м мн)	[u'sı]
beard	борода (ж)	[bara'da]
to have (a beard, etc.)	носить	[na'sitʲ]
braid	коса (ж)	[ka'sa]
sideburns	бакенбарды (мн)	[bakin'bardı]
red-haired (adj)	рыжий	['rıʒıj]
gray (hair)	седой	[si'dɔj]

| bald (adj) | лысый | ['lɪsɪj] |
| bald patch | лысина (ж) | ['lɪsinə] |

| ponytail | хвост (м) | [hvɔst] |
| bangs | чёлка (ж) | ['ʧɔlkə] |

62. Human body

| hand | кисть (ж) | [kistʲ] |
| arm | рука (ж) | [rʊ'ka] |

finger	палец (м)	['palets]
thumb	большой палец (м)	[baʌ'ʃɔj 'palets]
little finger	мизинец (м)	[mi'zinets]
nail	ноготь (м)	['nɔgatʲ]

fist	кулак (м)	[kʊ'lak]
palm	ладонь (ж)	[la'dɔn]
wrist	запястье (с)	[za'pʲasʲtje]
forearm	предплечье (с)	[pritp'letʃje]
elbow	локоть (м)	['lɔkatʲ]
shoulder	плечо (с)	[pli'ʧɔ]

leg	нога (ж)	[na'ga]
foot	ступня (ж)	[stʊp'ɲa]
knee	колено (с)	[ka'lenə]
calf (part of leg)	икра (ж)	[ik'ra]

| hip | бедро (с) | [bid'rɔ] |
| heel | пятка (ж) | ['pʲatkə] |

body	тело (с)	['telə]
stomach	живот (м)	[ʒɪ'vɔt]
chest	грудь (ж)	[grʊtʲ]
breast	грудь (ж)	[grʊtʲ]
flank	бок (м)	[bɔk]
back	спина (ж)	[spi'na]

| lower back | поясница (ж) | [pais'nitsə] |
| waist | талия (ж) | ['talija] |

navel (belly button)	пупок (м)	[pʊ'pɔk]
buttocks	ягодицы (мн)	[jaga'ditsɪ]
bottom	зад (м)	[zat]

beauty mark	родинка (ж)	['rɔdinkə]
birthmark (café au lait spot)	родимое пятно (с)	[ra'dimae pit'nɔ]
tattoo	татуировка (ж)	[tatʊi'rɔfkə]
scar	шрам (м)	[ʃram]

63. Diseases

sickness	болезнь (ж)	[ba'lezɲ]
to be sick	болеть	[ba'letʲ]
health	здоровье (с)	[zda'rɔvje]
runny nose (coryza)	насморк (м)	['nasmark]
tonsillitis	ангина (ж)	[a'ɲinə]
cold (illness)	простуда (ж)	[pras'tʊdə]
to catch a cold	простудиться	[prastʊ'ditsə]
bronchitis	бронхит (м)	[bran'hit]
pneumonia	воспаление (с) лёгких	[vaspa'lenie 'lɜĥkih]
flu, influenza	грипп (м)	[grip]
nearsighted (adj)	близорукий	[bliza'rʊkij]
farsighted (adj)	дальнозоркий	[daʎna'zorkij]
strabismus (crossed eyes)	косоглазие (с)	[kasag'lazie]
cross-eyed (adj)	косоглазый	[kasag'lazɪj]
cataract	катаракта (ж)	[kata'raktə]
glaucoma	глаукома (ж)	[glau'kɔmə]
stroke	инсульт (м)	[in'sʊʎt]
heart attack	инфаркт (м)	[in'farkt]
myocardial infarction	инфаркт (м) миокарда	[in'farkt mia'kardə]
paralysis	паралич (м)	[para'litʃ]
to paralyze (vt)	парализовать	[paraliza'vatʲ]
allergy	аллергия (ж)	[alir'gija]
asthma	астма (ж)	['astmə]
diabetes	диабет (м)	[dia'bet]
toothache	зубная боль (ж)	[zub'naja bɔʎ]
caries	кариес (м)	['karies]
diarrhea	диарея (ж)	[dia'reja]
constipation	запор (м)	[za'por]
stomach upset	расстройство (с) желудка	[rast'rojstva ʒɛ'lutkə]
food poisoning	отравление (с)	[atrav'lenie]
to get food poisoning	отравиться	[atra'witsə]
arthritis	артрит (м)	[art'rit]
rickets	рахит (м)	[ra'hit]
rheumatism	ревматизм (м)	[rivma'tizm]
atherosclerosis	атеросклероз (м)	[ateraskle'rɔs]
gastritis	гастрит (м)	[gast'rit]
appendicitis	аппендицит (м)	[apindi'tsɪt]
cholecystitis	холецистит (м)	[haletsɪs'tit]
ulcer	язва (ж)	['jazvə]

measles	корь (ж)	[kɔrʲ]
rubella (German measles)	краснуха (ж)	[kras'nʊhə]
jaundice	желтуха (ж)	[ʒɛl'tʊhə]
hepatitis	гепатит (м)	[gipa'tit]

schizophrenia	шизофрения (ж)	[ʃɪzafre'nija]
rabies (hydrophobia)	бешенство (с)	['beʃənstvə]
neurosis	невроз (м)	[niv'rɔs]
concussion	сотрясение (с) мозга	[satri'senie 'mɔzgə]

cancer	рак (м)	[rak]
sclerosis	склероз (м)	[skle'rɔs]
multiple sclerosis	рассеянный склероз (м)	[ra'seinɪj skle'rɔs]

alcoholism	алкоголизм (м)	[alkaga'lizm]
alcoholic (n)	алкоголик (м)	[alka'gɔlik]
syphilis	сифилис (м)	['sifilis]
AIDS	СПИД (м)	[spit]

tumor	опухоль (ж)	['ɔpʊhaʎ]
malignant (adj)	злокачественная	[zla'katʃestwenaja]
benign (adj)	доброкачественная	[dabra'katʃestwenaja]

fever	лихорадка (ж)	[liha'ratkə]
malaria	малярия (ж)	[mali'rija]
gangrene	гангрена (ж)	[gahg'renə]
seasickness	морская болезнь (ж)	[mars'kaja ba'lezɲ]
epilepsy	эпилепсия (ж)	[ɛpi'lepsija]

epidemic	эпидемия (ж)	[ɛpi'demija]
typhus	тиф (м)	[tif]
tuberculosis	туберкулёз (м)	[tʊberkʊ'lɜs]
cholera	холера (ж)	[ha'lerə]
plague (bubonic ~)	чума (ж)	['ʧumə]

64. Symptoms. Treatments. Part 1

symptom	симптом (м)	[simp'tɔm]
temperature	температура (ж)	[timpera'tʊrə]
high temperature (fever)	высокая температура (ж)	[vɪ'sɔkaja timpera'tʊrə]
pulse	пульс (м)	[pʊʎs]

dizziness (vertigo)	головокружение (с)	[galavakrʊ'ʒenie]
hot (adj)	горячий	[ga'rʲatʃij]
shivering	озноб (м)	[az'nɔp]
pale (e.g., ~ face)	бледный	[b'lednɪj]

| cough | кашель (м) | ['kaʃəʎ] |
| to cough (vi) | кашлять | ['kaʃlitʲ] |

to sneeze (vi)	**чихать**	[ʧi'hatʲ]
faint	**обморок** (м)	['ɔbmarak]
to faint (vi)	**упасть в обморок**	[u'pastʲ v 'ɔbmarak]
bruise (hématome)	**синяк** (м)	[si'ɲak]
bump (lump)	**шишка** (ж)	['ʃiʃkə]
to bang (bump)	**удариться**	[u'daritsə]
contusion (bruise)	**ушиб** (м)	[u'ʃip]
to get a bruise	**ударить …**	[u'daritʲ]
to limp (vi)	**хромать**	[hra'matʲ]
dislocation	**вывих** (м)	['vɪwih]
to dislocate (vt)	**вывихнуть**	['vɪwihnʊtʲ]
fracture	**перелом** (м)	[pere'lɔm]
to have a fracture	**получить перелом**	[palu'ʧitʲ pere'lɔm]
cut (e.g., paper ~)	**порез** (м)	[pa'res]
to cut oneself	**порезаться**	[pa'rezatsə]
bleeding	**кровотечение** (с)	[kravate'ʧenie]
burn (injury)	**ожог** (м)	[a'ʒɔk]
to get burned	**обжечься**	[ab'ʒeʧsʲa]
to prick (vt)	**уколоть**	[uka'lɔtʲ]
to prick oneself	**уколоться**	[uka'lɔtsə]
to injure (vt)	**повредить**	[pavre'ditʲ]
injury	**повреждение** (с)	[pavreʒ'denie]
wound	**рана** (ж)	['ranə]
trauma	**травма** (ж)	[t'ravmə]
to be delirious	**бредить**	[b'reditʲ]
to stutter (vi)	**заикаться**	[zai'katsə]
sunstroke	**солнечный удар** (м)	['sɔlniʧnɪj u'dar]

65. Symptoms. Treatments. Part 2

pain	**боль** (ж)	[bɔʎ]
splinter (in foot, etc.)	**заноза** (ж)	[za'nɔzə]
sweat (perspiration)	**пот** (м)	[pɔt]
to sweat (perspire)	**потеть**	[pa'tetʲ]
vomiting	**рвота** (ж)	[r'vɔtə]
convulsions	**судороги** (ж мн)	['sʊdaragi]
pregnant (adj)	**беременная**	[bi'remenaja]
to be born	**родиться**	[ra'ditsə]
delivery, labor	**роды** (мн)	['rɔdɪ]
to deliver (~ a baby)	**рожать**	[ra'ʒatʲ]
abortion	**аборт** (м)	[a'bɔrt]
breathing, respiration	**дыхание** (с)	[dɪ'hanie]

in-breath (inhalation)	вдох (м)	[vdɔh]
out-breath (exhalation)	выдох (м)	['vɪdah]
to exhale (breathe out)	выдохнуть	['vɪdahnʊtʲ]
to inhale (vi)	сделать вдох	[s'delatʲ vdɔh]

disabled person	инвалид (м)	[inva'lit]
cripple	калека (с)	[ka'lekə]
drug addict	наркоман (м)	[narka'man]

deaf (adj)	глухой	[glu'hɔj]
mute (adj)	немой	[ni'mɔj]
deaf mute (adj)	глухонемой	[gluhani'mɔj]

mad, insane (adj)	сумасшедший	[sʊma'ʃətʃij]
madman (demented person)	сумасшедший (м)	[sʊma'ʃətʃij]
madwoman	сумасшедшая (ж)	[sʊma'ʃətʃʌja]
to go insane	сойти с ума	[saj'ti sʊ'ma]

gene	ген (м)	[gen]
immunity	иммунитет (м)	[imʊni'tet]
hereditary (adj)	наследственный	[nas'letstwennɪj]
congenital (adj)	врождённый	[vraʒ'dɔnnɪj]

virus	вирус (м)	['wirʊs]
microbe	микроб (м)	[mik'rɔp]
bacterium	бактерия (ж)	[bak'tɛrija]
infection	инфекция (ж)	[in'fektsɪja]

66. Symptoms. Treatments. Part 3

| hospital | больница (ж) | [baʎ'nitsə] |
| patient | пациент (м) | [patsɪ'ɛnt] |

diagnosis	диагноз (м)	[di'agnas]
cure	лечение (с)	[li'tʃenie]
medical treatment	лечение (с)	[li'tʃenie]
to get treatment	лечиться	[li'tʃitsə]
to treat (~ a patient)	лечить	[li'tʃitʲ]
to nurse (look after)	ухаживать	[u'haʒɪvatʲ]
care (nursing ~)	уход (м)	[u'hɔt]

operation, surgery	операция (ж)	[api'ratsɪja]
to bandage (head, limb)	перевязать	[pirewi'zatʲ]
bandaging	перевязка (ж)	[pire'vʲaskə]

vaccination	прививка (ж)	[pri'wifkə]
to vaccinate (vt)	делать прививку	['delatʲ pri'wifkʊ]
injection, shot	укол (м)	[u'kɔl]
to give an injection	делать укол	['delatʲ u'kɔl]

amputation	ампутация (ж)	[ampʊ'tatsɪja]
to amputate (vt)	ампутировать	[ampʊ'tiravatʲ]
coma	кома (ж)	['kɔmə]
to be in a coma	быть в коме	[bɪtʲ f 'kɔme]
intensive care	реанимация (ж)	[riani'matsɪja]

to recover (~ from flu)	выздоравливать	[vɪzda'ravlivatʲ]
condition (patient's ~)	состояние (с)	[sasta'janie]
consciousness	сознание (с)	[saz'nanie]
memory (faculty)	память (ж)	['pamitʲ]

to pull out (tooth)	удалять	[uda'ʎatʲ]
filling	пломба (ж)	[p'lɔmbə]
to fill (a tooth)	пломбировать	[plambira'vatʲ]

| hypnosis | гипноз (м) | [gip'nɔs] |
| to hypnotize (vt) | гипнотизировать | [gipnati'ziravatʲ] |

67. Medicine. Drugs. Accessories

medicine, drug	лекарство (с)	[li'karstvə]
remedy	средство (с)	[s'retstvə]
to prescribe (vt)	прописать	[prapi'satʲ]
prescription	рецепт (м)	[ri'tsəpt]

tablet, pill	таблетка (ж)	[tab'letkə]
ointment	мазь (ж)	[masʲ]
ampule	ампула (ж)	['ampʊlə]
mixture	микстура (ж)	[miks'tʊrə]
syrup	сироп (м)	[si'rop]
pill	пилюля (ж)	[pi'lyʎa]
powder	порошок (м)	[para'ʃok]

gauze bandage	бинт (м)	[bint]
cotton wool	вата (ж)	['vatə]
iodine	йод (м)	[jot]

Band-Aid	лейкопластырь (м)	[lejkap'lastɪrʲ]
eyedropper	пипетка (ж)	[pi'petkə]
thermometer	градусник (м)	[g'radʊsnik]
syringe	шприц (м)	[ʃprits]

| wheelchair | коляска (ж) | [ka'ʎaskə] |
| crutches | костыли (м мн) | [kastɪ'li] |

painkiller	обезболивающее (с)	[abiz'bolivajuɕee]
laxative	слабительное (с)	[sla'biteʎnae]
spirits (ethanol)	спирт (м)	[spirt]
medicinal herbs	трава (ж)	[tra'va]
herbal (~ tea)	травяной	[trawi'noj]

APARTMENT

T&P Books Publishing

68. Apartment

apartment	квартира (ж)	[kvar'tirə]
room	комната (ж)	['kɔmnatə]
bedroom	спальня (ж)	[s'paʎɲa]
dining room	столовая (ж)	[sta'lɔvaja]
living room	гостиная (ж)	[gas'tinaja]
study (home office)	кабинет (м)	[kabi'net]
entry room	прихожая (ж)	[pri'hɔʒaja]
bathroom (room with a bath or shower)	ванная комната (ж)	['vannaja 'kɔmnatə]
half bath	туалет (м)	[tʊa'let]
ceiling	потолок (м)	[pata'lɔk]
floor	пол (м)	[pɔl]
corner	угол (м)	['ugal]

69. Furniture. Interior

furniture	мебель (ж)	['mebeʎ]
table	стол (м)	[stɔl]
chair	стул (м)	[stʊl]
bed	кровать (ж)	[kra'vatʲ]
couch, sofa	диван (м)	[di'van]
armchair	кресло (с)	[k'reslə]
bookcase	книжный шкаф (м)	[k'niʒnij ʃkaf]
shelf	полка (ж)	['pɔlkə]
shelving unit	этажерка (ж)	[ɛta'ʒɛrkə]
wardrobe	гардероб (м)	[garde'rɔp]
coat rack (wall-mounted ~)	вешалка (ж)	['weʃʌlkə]
coat stand	вешалка (ж)	['weʃʌlkə]
bureau, dresser	комод (м)	[ka'mɔt]
coffee table	журнальный столик (м)	[ʒur'naʎnij s'tɔlik]
mirror	зеркало (с)	['zerkalə]
carpet	ковёр (м)	[ka'wзr]
rug, small carpet	коврик (м)	['kɔvrik]
fireplace	камин (м)	[ka'min]
candle	свеча (ж)	[swi'ʧa]

candlestick	подсвечник (м)	[pats'wetʃnik]
drapes	шторы (ж мн)	[ʃ'tɔrɪ]
wallpaper	обои (мн)	[a'bɔi]
blinds (jalousie)	жалюзи (мн)	[ʒaly'zi]

table lamp	настольная лампа (ж)	[nas'tɔʌnaja 'lampə]
wall lamp (sconce)	светильник (м)	[swi'tiʌnik]
floor lamp	торшер (м)	[tar'ʃer]
chandelier	люстра (ж)	['lystrə]

leg (of chair, table)	ножка (ж)	['nɔʃkə]
armrest	подлокотник (м)	[padla'kɔtnik]
back (backrest)	спинка (ж)	[s'pinkə]
drawer	ящик (м)	['jaɕik]

70. Bedding

bedclothes	постельное бельё	[pas'teʌnae bi'ʎjo]
pillow	подушка (ж)	[pa'duʃkə]
pillowcase	наволочка (ж)	['navalatʃkə]
duvet, comforter	одеяло (c)	[adi'jalə]
sheet	простыня (ж)	[prastɪ'ɲa]
bedspread	покрывало (c)	[pakrɪ'valə]

71. Kitchen

kitchen	кухня (ж)	['kʋhɲa]
gas	газ (м)	[gas]
gas stove (range)	газовая плита (ж)	['gazavaja pli'ta]
electric stove	электроплита (ж)	[ɛlektrapli'ta]
oven	духовка (ж)	[dʋ'hɔfkə]
microwave oven	микроволновая печь (ж)	[mikraval'nɔvaja petʃ]

refrigerator	холодильник (м)	[hala'diʌnik]
freezer	морозильник (м)	[mara'ziʌnik]
dishwasher	посудомоечная машина (ж)	[pasʋda'mɔetʃnaja ma'ʃinə]

meat grinder	мясорубка (ж)	[misa'rʋpkə]
juicer	соковыжималка (ж)	[sɔkavɪʒɪ'malkə]
toaster	тостер (м)	['tɔster]
mixer	миксер (м)	['mikser]

coffee machine	кофеварка (ж)	[kafe'varkə]
coffee pot	кофейник (м)	[ka'fejnik]
coffee grinder	кофемолка (ж)	[kafe'mɔlkə]
kettle	чайник (м)	['tʃajnik]
teapot	чайник (м)	['tʃajnik]

| lid | крышка (ж) | [k'rɪʃkə] |
| tea strainer | ситечко (с) | ['sitetʃkə] |

spoon	ложка (ж)	['lɔʃkə]
teaspoon	чайная ложка (ж)	['tʃajnaja 'lɔʃkə]
soup spoon	столовая ложка (ж)	[sta'lɔvaja 'lɔʃkə]
fork	вилка (ж)	['wilkə]
knife	нож (м)	[nɔʃ]

tableware (dishes)	посуда (ж)	[pa'sʊdə]
plate (dinner ~)	тарелка (ж)	[ta'relkə]
saucer	блюдце (с)	[b'lytse]

shot glass	рюмка (ж)	['rymkə]
glass (tumbler)	стакан (м)	[sta'kan]
cup	чашка (ж)	['tʃaʃkə]

sugar bowl	сахарница (ж)	['saharnitsə]
salt shaker	солонка (ж)	[sa'lɔnkə]
pepper shaker	перечница (ж)	['peretʃnitsə]
butter dish	маслёнка (ж)	[mas'lɔnkə]

stock pot (soup pot)	кастрюля (ж)	[kast'ryʎa]
frying pan (skillet)	сковородка (ж)	[skava'rɔtkə]
ladle	половник (м)	[pa'lɔvnik]
colander	дуршлаг (м)	[dʊrʃ'lak]
tray (serving ~)	поднос (м)	[pad'nɔs]

bottle	бутылка (ж)	[bʊ'tɪlkə]
jar (glass)	банка (ж)	['bankə]
can	банка (ж)	['bankə]

bottle opener	открывалка (ж)	[atkrɪ'valkə]
can opener	открывалка (ж)	[atkrɪ'valkə]
corkscrew	штопор (м)	[ʃ'tɔpar]
filter	фильтр (м)	[fiʎtr]
to filter (vt)	фильтровать	[fiʎtra'vatʲ]

| trash, garbage (food waste, etc.) | мусор (м) | ['mʊsar] |
| trash can (kitchen ~) | мусорное ведро (с) | ['mʊsarnae wid'rɔ] |

72. Bathroom

bathroom	ванная комната (ж)	['vannaja 'kɔmnatə]
water	вода (ж)	[va'da]
faucet	кран (м)	[kran]
hot water	горячая вода (ж)	[ga'rʲatʃaja va'da]
cold water	холодная вода (ж)	[ha'lɔdnaja va'da]
toothpaste	зубная паста (ж)	[zub'naja 'pastə]

| to brush one's teeth | чистить зубы | ['t͡ʃistit͡ʲ 'zubɪ] |
| toothbrush | зубная щётка (ж) | [zub'naja 'ɕɜtkə] |

to shave (vi)	бриться	[b'ritsə]
shaving foam	пена (ж) для бритья	['penə dʎa bri'tja]
razor	бритва (ж)	[b'ritvə]

to wash (one's hands, etc.)	мыть	[mɪtʲ]
to take a bath	мыться	['mɪtsə]
shower	душ (м)	[duʃ]
to take a shower	принимать душ	[prini'matʲ duʃ]

bathtub	ванна (ж)	['vɑnnə]
toilet (toilet bowl)	унитаз (м)	[uni'tas]
sink (washbasin)	раковина (ж)	['rɑkawinə]

| soap | мыло (с) | ['mɪlə] |
| soap dish | мыльница (ж) | ['mɪʎnitsə] |

sponge	губка (ж)	['gupkə]
shampoo	шампунь (м)	[ʃʌm'puɲ]
towel	полотенце (с)	[pɑlɑ'tentse]
bathrobe	халат (м)	[hɑ'lat]

laundry (process)	стирка (ж)	[s'tirkə]
washing machine	стиральная машина (ж)	[sti'raʎnaja ma'ʃinə]
to do the laundry	стирать бельё	[sti'ratʲ be'ʎjo]
laundry detergent	стиральный порошок (м)	[sti'raʎnij pɑrɑ'ʃɔk]

73. Household appliances

TV set	телевизор (м)	[tile'wizar]
tape recorder	магнитофон (м)	[mɑgnitɑ'fɔn]
VCR (video recorder)	видеомагнитофон (м)	['widea mɑgnitɑ'fɔn]
radio	приёмник (м)	[pri3mnik]
player (CD, MP3, etc.)	плеер (м)	[p'lɛer]

video projector	видеопроектор (м)	['widea prɑ'ektar]
home movie theater	домашний кинотеатр (м)	[dɑ'maʃnij kinate'atr]
DVD player	DVD проигрыватель (м)	[diwi'di prɑ'igrɪvateʎ]
amplifier	усилитель (м)	[usi'liteʎ]
video game console	игровая приставка (ж)	[igra'vaja pris'tafkə]

video camera	видеокамера (ж)	[widea'kamerə]
camera (photo)	фотоаппарат (м)	[fɔtɑpɑ'rat]
digital camera	цифровой фотоаппарат (м)	[tsɪfra'vɔj fɔtɑpɑ'rat]

| vacuum cleaner | пылесос (м) | [pɪle'sɔs] |
| iron (e.g., steam ~) | утюг (м) | [u'tyk] |

ironing board	гладильная доска (ж)	[glɑˈdiʎnɑja dɑsˈkɑ]
telephone	телефон (м)	[tileˈfɔn]
mobile phone	мобильный телефон (м)	[mɑˈbiʎnɪj teleˈfɔn]
sewing machine	швейная машинка (ж)	[ʃˈwejnɑja mɑˈʃinkə]
microphone	микрофон (м)	[mikrɑˈfɔn]
headphones	наушники (м мн)	[nɑˈuʃniki]
remote control (TV)	пульт (м)	[puʎt]
CD, compact disc	компакт-диск (м)	[kɑmˈpɑkt ˈdisk]
cassette	кассета (ж)	[kɑˈsetə]
vinyl record	пластинка (ж)	[plɑsˈtinkə]

THE EARTH. WEATHER

T&P Books Publishing

space	космос (м)	['kɔsmas]
space (as adj)	космический	[kas'mitʃeskij]
outer space	космическое пространство	[kas'mitʃeskae prast'ranstvə]
world	мир (м)	[mir]
universe	вселенная (ж)	[fsi'lennaja]
galaxy	галактика (ж)	[ga'laktikə]
star	звезда (ж)	[zwez'da]
constellation	созвездие (с)	[saz'wezdie]
planet	планета (ж)	[pla'netə]
satellite	спутник (м)	[s'putnik]
meteorite	метеорит (м)	[mitea'rit]
comet	комета (ж)	[ka'metə]
asteroid	астероид (м)	[aste'rɔit]
orbit	орбита (ж)	[ar'bitə]
to revolve (~ around the Earth)	вращаться	[vra'ɕatsə]
atmosphere	атмосфера (ж)	[atmas'ferə]
the Sun	Солнце (с)	['sɔntsе]
solar system	Солнечная система (ж)	['sɔlnitʃnaja sis'temə]
solar eclipse	солнечное затмение (с)	['sɔlnitʃnae zat'menie]
the Earth	Земля (ж)	[zem'ʎa]
the Moon	Луна (ж)	['lunə]
Mars	Марс (м)	[mars]
Venus	Венера (ж)	[wi'nerə]
Jupiter	Юпитер (м)	[ju'piter]
Saturn	Сатурн (м)	[sa'turn]
Mercury	Меркурий (м)	[mir'kurij]
Uranus	Уран (м)	[u'ran]
Neptune	Нептун (м)	[nip'tun]
Pluto	Плутон (м)	[plu'tɔn]
Milky Way	Млечный Путь (м)	[m'letʃnɪj putʲ]
Great Bear (Ursa Major)	Большая Медведица (ж)	[baʎ'ʃaja mid'weditsə]
North Star	Полярная Звезда (ж)	[pa'ʎarnaja zwez'da]
Martian	марсианин (м)	[marsi'anin]
extraterrestrial (n)	инопланетянин (м)	[inaplani'tʲanin]

| alien | пришелец (м) | [priˈʃɛlets] |
| flying saucer | летающая тарелка (ж) | [leˈtajuɕeja taˈrelkə] |

spaceship	космический корабль (м)	[kasˈmitʃeskij kaˈrabʎ]
space station	орбитальная станция (ж)	[arbiˈtaʎnaja sˈtantsija]
blast-off	старт (м)	[start]

engine	двигатель (м)	[dˈwigateʎ]
nozzle	сопло (с)	[ˈsɔplə]
fuel	топливо (с)	[ˈtɔplivə]

cockpit, flight deck	кабина (ж)	[kaˈbinə]
antenna	антенна (ж)	[anˈtɛnə]
porthole	иллюминатор (м)	[ilymiˈnatar]
solar panel	солнечная батарея (ж)	[ˈsɔlnetʃnaja bataˈreja]
spacesuit	скафандр (м)	[skaˈfandr]

| weightlessness | невесомость (ж) | [niwiˈsɔmastʲ] |
| oxygen | кислород (м) | [kislaˈrɔt] |

| docking (in space) | стыковка (ж) | [stɪˈkɔfkə] |
| to dock (vi, vt) | производить стыковку | [praizvaˈditʲ stɪˈkɔfkʊ] |

observatory	обсерватория (ж)	[apservaˈtɔrija]
telescope	телескоп (м)	[tilesˈkɔp]
to observe (vt)	наблюдать	[nablyˈdatʲ]
to explore (vt)	исследовать	[isˈledavatʲ]

75. The Earth

the Earth	Земля (ж)	[zemˈʎa]
the globe (the Earth)	земной шар (м)	[zemˈnɔj ʃʌr]
planet	планета (ж)	[plaˈnetə]

atmosphere	атмосфера (ж)	[atmasˈferə]
geography	география (ж)	[giagˈrafija]
nature	природа (ж)	[priˈrɔdə]

globe (table ~)	глобус (м)	[gˈlɔbʊs]
map	карта (ж)	[ˈkartə]
atlas	атлас (м)	[ˈatlas]

Europe	Европа (ж)	[evˈrɔpə]
Asia	Азия (ж)	[ˈazija]
Africa	Африка (ж)	[ˈafrikə]
Australia	Австралия (ж)	[afstˈralija]
America	Америка (ж)	[aˈmerikə]
North America	Северная Америка (ж)	[ˈsewernaja aˈmerikə]

South America	Южная Америка (ж)	['juʒnaja a'merikə]
Antarctica	Антарктида (ж)	[antark'tidə]
the Arctic	Арктика (ж)	['arktikə]

76. Cardinal directions

north	север (м)	['sewer]
to the north	на север	[na 'sewer]
in the north	на севере	[na 'sewere]
northern (adj)	северный	['sewernıj]

south	юг (м)	[juk]
to the south	на юг	[na 'juk]
in the south	на юге	[na 'juge]
southern (adj)	южный	['juʒnıj]

west	запад (м)	['zapat]
to the west	на запад	[na 'zapat]
in the west	на западе	[na 'zapade]
western (adj)	западный	['zapadnıj]

east	восток (м)	[vas'tɔk]
to the east	на восток	[na vas'tɔk]
in the east	на востоке	[na vas'tɔke]
eastern (adj)	восточный	[vas'tɔtʃnıj]

77. Sea. Ocean

sea	море (с)	['mɔre]
ocean	океан (м)	[aki'an]
gulf (bay)	залив (м)	[za'lif]
straits	пролив (м)	[pra'lif]

land (solid ground)	земля (ж), суша (ж)	[zem'ʎa], ['suʃe]
continent (mainland)	материк (м)	[mate'rik]
island	остров (м)	['ɔstraf]
peninsula	полуостров (м)	[palu'ɔstraf]
archipelago	архипелаг (м)	[arhipe'lak]

bay, cove	бухта (ж)	['buhtə]
harbor	гавань (ж)	['gavaɲ]
lagoon	лагуна (ж)	[la'gunə]
cape	мыс (м)	[mıs]

atoll	атолл (м)	[a'tɔl]
reef	риф (м)	[rif]
coral	коралл (м)	[ka'ral]
coral reef	коралловый риф (м)	[ka'ralavıj rif]

deep (adj)	глубокий	[glu'bɔkij]
depth (deep water)	глубина (ж)	[glubi'na]
abyss	бездна (ж)	['bɛznə]
trench (e.g., Mariana ~)	впадина (ж)	[fʲpadinə]
current (Ocean ~)	течение (с)	[ti'tʃenie]
to surround (bathe)	омывать	[amɪ'vatʲ]
shore	побережье	[pabi'reʒje]
coast	берег (м)	['berek]
flow (flood tide)	прилив (м)	[pri'lif]
ebb (ebb tide)	отлив (м)	[at'lif]
shoal	отмель (ж)	['ɔtmeʎ]
bottom (~ of the sea)	дно (с)	[dnɔ]
wave	волна (ж)	[val'na]
crest (~ of a wave)	гребень (м) волны	[g'rebeɲ val'nɪ]
spume (sea foam)	пена (ж)	['penə]
storm (sea storm)	буря (ж)	['burʲa]
hurricane	ураган (м)	[ura'gan]
tsunami	цунами (с)	[tsu'nami]
calm (dead ~)	штиль (м)	[ʃtiʎ]
quiet, calm (adj)	спокойный	[spa'kɔjnɪj]
pole	полюс (м)	['pɔlys]
polar (adj)	полярный	[pa'ʎarnɪj]
latitude	широта (ж)	[ʃira'ta]
longitude	долгота (ж)	[dalga'ta]
parallel	параллель (ж)	[para'leʎ]
equator	экватор (м)	[ɛk'vatar]
sky	небо (с)	['nebə]
horizon	горизонт (м)	[gari'zɔnt]
air	воздух (м)	['vɔzdʊh]
lighthouse	маяк (м)	[ma'jak]
to dive (vi)	нырять	[nɪ'rʲatʲ]
to sink (ab. boat)	затонуть	[zata'nʊtʲ]
treasures	сокровища (мн)	[sak'rɔwiɕə]

78. Seas' and Oceans' names

Atlantic Ocean	Атлантический океан (м)	[atlan'titʃeskij aki'an]
Indian Ocean	Индийский океан (м)	[in'dijskij aki'an]
Pacific Ocean	Тихий океан (м)	['tihij aki'an]
Arctic Ocean	Северный Ледовитый океан (м)	['sewernɪj leda'witɪj aki'an]

Black Sea	Чёрное море (c)	['tʃɔrnae 'mɔre]
Red Sea	Красное море (c)	[k'rasnae 'mɔre]
Yellow Sea	Желтое море (c)	['ʒɔltae 'mɔre]
White Sea	Белое море (c)	['belae 'mɔre]

Caspian Sea	Каспийское море (c)	[kas'pijskae 'mɔre]
Dead Sea	Мёртвое море (c)	['mɜrtvae 'mɔre]
Mediterranean Sea	Средиземное море (c)	[sredi'zemnae 'mɔre]

| Aegean Sea | Эгейское море (c) | [ɛ'gejskae 'mɔre] |
| Adriatic Sea | Адриатическое море (c) | [adria'titʃeskae 'mɔre] |

Arabian Sea	Аравийское море (c)	[ara'wijskae 'mɔre]
Sea of Japan	Японское море (c)	[ja'ponskae 'mɔre]
Bering Sea	Берингово море (c)	['berihgava 'mɔre]
South China Sea	Южно-Китайское море (c)	['juʒna ki'tajskae 'mɔre]

Coral Sea	Коралловое море (c)	[ka'ralavae 'mɔre]
Tasman Sea	Тасманово море (c)	[tas'manava 'mɔre]
Caribbean Sea	Карибское море (c)	[ka'ripskae 'mɔre]

| Barents Sea | Баренцево море (c) | ['barintsəva 'mɔre] |
| Kara Sea | Карское море (c) | ['karskae 'mɔre] |

North Sea	Северное море (c)	['sewernae 'mɔre]
Baltic Sea	Балтийское море (c)	[bal'tijskae 'mɔre]
Norwegian Sea	Норвежское море (c)	[nar'weʃskae 'mɔre]

79. Mountains

mountain	гора (ж)	[ga'ra]
mountain range	горная цепь (ж)	['gornaja tsəpʲ]
mountain ridge	горный хребет (м)	['gornij hre'bet]

summit, top	вершина (ж)	[wir'ʃinə]
peak	пик (м)	[pik]
foot (~ of the mountain)	подножие (c)	[pad'noʒɪe]
slope (mountainside)	склон (м)	[sklɔn]

volcano	вулкан (м)	[vʊl'kan]
active volcano	действующий вулкан (м)	['dejstvʊɕij vʊl'kan]
dormant volcano	потухший вулкан (м)	[pa'tʊhʃij vʊl'kan]

eruption	извержение (c)	[izwer'ʒɛnie]
crater	кратер (м)	[k'rater]
magma	магма (ж)	['magmə]
lava	лава (ж)	['lavə]
molten (~ lava)	раскалённый	[raska'lɔnnɪj]

canyon	каньон (м)	[ka'njon]
gorge	ущелье (с)	[u'ɕeʌje]
crevice	расщелина (ж)	[ra'ɕelinə]
pass, col	перевал (м)	[pere'val]
plateau	плато (с)	[pla'tɔ]
cliff	скала (ж)	[ska'la]
hill	холм (м)	[hɔlm]
glacier	ледник (м)	[lid'nik]
waterfall	водопад (м)	[vada'pat]
geyser	гейзер (м)	['gejzer]
lake	озеро (с)	['ɔzerə]
plain	равнина (ж)	[rav'ninə]
landscape	пейзаж (м)	[pij'zaʃ]
echo	эхо (с)	['ɛhə]
alpinist	альпинист (м)	[aʌpi'nist]
rock climber	скалолаз (м)	[skala'las]
to conquer (in climbing)	покорять	[paka'rʲatʲ]
climb (an easy ~)	восхождение (с)	[vashaʒ'denie]

80. Mountains names

The Alps	Альпы (мн)	['aʌpɪ]
Mont Blanc	Монблан (м)	[manb'lan]
The Pyrenees	Пиренеи (мн)	[pire'nei]
The Carpathians	Карпаты (мн)	[kar'patɪ]
The Ural Mountains	Уральские горы (мн)	[u'raʌskie 'gɔrɪ]
The Caucasus Mountains	Кавказ (м)	[kaf'kas]
Mount Elbrus	Эльбрус (м)	[ɛʌb'rʊs]
The Altai Mountains	Алтай (м)	[al'taj]
The Tian Shan	Тянь-Шань (ж)	[tʲaɲ 'ʃʌɲ]
The Pamir Mountains	Памир (м)	[pa'mir]
The Himalayas	Гималаи (мн)	[gima'lai]
Mount Everest	Эверест (м)	[ɛwi'rest]
The Andes	Анды (мн)	['andɪ]
Mount Kilimanjaro	Килиманджаро (ж)	[kiliman'ʒarə]

81. Rivers

river	река (ж)	[ri'ka]
spring (natural source)	источник (м)	[is'tɔtʃnik]
riverbed (river channel)	русло (с)	['rʊslə]

| basin | бассейн (м) | [ba'sɛjn] |
| to flow into … | впадать в … | [fpa'datʲ v] |

| tributary | приток (м) | [pri'tɔk] |
| bank (of river) | берег (м) | ['berek] |

current (stream)	течение (с)	[ti'tʃenie]
downstream (adv)	вниз по течению	[vnis pa ti'tʃeniju]
upstream (adv)	вверх по течению	[werh pa ti'tʃeniju]

inundation	наводнение (с)	[navad'nenie]
flooding	половодье (с)	[pala'vodje]
to overflow (vi)	разливаться	[razli'vatsə]
to flood (vt)	затоплять	[zatap'ʎatʲ]

| shallow (shoal) | мель (ж) | [meʎ] |
| rapids | порог (м) | [pa'rɔk] |

dam	плотина (ж)	[pla'tinə]
canal	канал (м)	[ka'nal]
reservoir (artificial lake)	водохранилище (с)	[vadahra'niliɕe]
sluice, lock	шлюз (м)	[ʃlys]

water body (pond, etc.)	водоём (м)	[vadaɜm]
swamp (marshland)	болото (с)	[ba'lɔtə]
bog, marsh	трясина (ж)	[tri'sinə]
whirlpool	водоворот (м)	[vadava'rɔt]

stream (brook)	ручей (м)	[rʊ'tʃej]
drinking (ab. water)	питьевой	[pitje'vɔj]
fresh (~ water)	пресный	[p'resnɪj]

| ice | лёд (м) | ['lɔt] |
| to freeze over (ab. river, etc.) | замёрзнуть | [za'mɜrznʊtʲ] |

82. Rivers' names

| Seine | Сена (ж) | ['senə] |
| Loire | Луара (ж) | [lu'arə] |

Thames	Темза (ж)	['tɛmzə]
Rhine	Рейн (м)	[rɛjn]
Danube	Дунай (м)	[dʊ'naj]

Volga	Волга (ж)	['vɔlgə]
Don	Дон (м)	[dɔn]
Lena	Лена (ж)	['lenə]
Yellow River	Хуанхэ (ж)	[hʊan'hɛ]
Yangtze	Янцзы (ж)	[jan'zɪ]

Mekong	**Меконг** (м)	[mi'kɔnk]
Ganges	**Ганг** (м)	[gɑnk]
Nile River	**Нил** (м)	[nil]
Congo River	**Конго** (ж)	['kɔhgə]
Okavango River	**Окаванго** (ж)	[ɑkɑ'vɑhgə]
Zambezi River	**Замбези** (ж)	[zɑm'bezi]
Limpopo River	**Лимпопо** (ж)	[lim'pɔpɔ]
Mississippi River	**Миссисипи** (ж)	[misi'sipi]

83. Forest

forest, wood	**лес** (м)	[les]
forest (as adj)	**лесной**	[lis'nɔj]
thick forest	**чаща** (ж)	['tʃaɕə]
grove	**роща** (ж)	['rɔɕə]
forest clearing	**поляна** (ж)	[pɑ'ʌanə]
thicket	**заросли** (мн)	['zɑrɑsli]
scrubland	**кустарник** (м)	[kʊs'tɑrnik]
footpath (troddenpath)	**тропинка** (ж)	[trɑ'pinkə]
gully	**овраг** (м)	[ɑv'rɑk]
tree	**дерево** (с)	['derevə]
leaf	**лист** (м)	[list]
leaves (foliage)	**листва** (ж)	[list'vɑ]
fall of leaves	**листопад** (м)	[listɑ'pɑt]
to fall (ab. leaves)	**опадать**	[ɑpɑ'dɑtʲ]
top (of the tree)	**верхушка** (ж)	[wir'hʊʃkə]
branch	**ветка** (ж)	['wetkə]
bough	**сук** (м)	[sʊk]
bud (on shrub, tree)	**почка** (ж)	['pɔtʃkə]
needle (of pine tree)	**игла** (ж)	[ig'lɑ]
pine cone	**шишка** (ж)	['ʃiʃkə]
hollow (in a tree)	**дупло** (с)	[dʊp'lɔ]
nest	**гнездо** (с)	[gniz'dɔ]
burrow (animal hole)	**нора** (ж)	[nɑ'rɑ]
trunk	**ствол** (м)	[stvɔl]
root	**корень** (м)	['kɔreɲ]
bark	**кора** (ж)	[kɑ'rɑ]
moss	**мох** (м)	[mɔh]
to uproot (remove trees or tree stumps)	**корчевать**	[kɑrtʃe'vɑtʲ]
to chop down	**рубить**	[rʊ'bitʲ]

| to deforest (vt) | вырубать лес | [vɪrʊ'batʲ les] |
| tree stump | пень (м) | [peɲ] |

campfire	костёр (м)	[kas'tɜr]
forest fire	пожар (м)	[pa'ʒar]
to extinguish (vt)	тушить	[tʊ'ʃitʲ]

forest ranger	лесник (м)	[lis'nik]
protection	охрана (ж)	[ah'ranə]
to protect (~ nature)	охранять	[ahra'ɲatʲ]

| poacher | браконьер (м) | [braka'ɲjer] |
| steel trap | капкан (м) | [kap'kan] |

| to gather, to pick (vt) | собирать | [sabi'ratʲ] |
| to lose one's way | заблудиться | [zablu'ditsə] |

84. Natural resources

natural resources	природные ресурсы (м мн)	[pri'rɔdnɪe re'sʊrsɪ]
minerals	полезные ископаемые (с мн)	[pa'leznɪe iska'paemɪe]
deposits	залежи (мн)	['zaleʒɪ]
field (e.g., oilfield)	месторождение (с)	[mistaraʒ'denie]

to mine (extract)	добывать	[dabɪ'vatʲ]
mining (extraction)	добыча (ж)	[da'bɪtʃə]
ore	руда (ж)	[rʊ'da]
mine (e.g., for coal)	рудник (м)	[rʊd'nik]
shaft (mine ~)	шахта (ж)	['ʃʌhtə]
miner	шахтёр (м)	[ʃʌh'tɜr]

| gas (natural ~) | газ (м) | [gas] |
| gas pipeline | газопровод (м) | [gazapra'vɔt] |

oil (petroleum)	нефть (ж)	[neftʲ]
oil pipeline	нефтепровод (м)	[neftepra'vɔt]
oil well	нефтяная вышка (ж)	[nefti'naja 'vɪʃkə]
derrick (tower)	буровая вышка (ж)	[bʊra'vaja 'vɪʃkə]
tanker	танкер (м)	['tanker]

sand	песок (м)	[pi'sɔk]
limestone	известняк (м)	[izwes'ɲak]
gravel	гравий (м)	[g'rawij]
peat	торф (м)	[tɔrf]
clay	глина (ж)	[g'linə]
coal	уголь (м)	['ugaʎ]
iron (ore)	железо (с)	[ʒɪ'lezə]
gold	золото (с)	['zɔlatə]

silver	серебро (с)	[sirib'rɔ]
nickel	никель (м)	['nikeʎ]
copper	медь (ж)	[metʲ]

zinc	цинк (м)	[ʦınk]
manganese	марганец (м)	['marganeʦ]
mercury	ртуть (ж)	[rtʊtʲ]
lead	свинец (м)	[swi'neʦ]

mineral	минерал (м)	[mine'ral]
crystal	кристалл (м)	[kris'tal]
marble	мрамор (м)	[m'ramar]
uranium	уран (м)	[u'ran]

85. Weather

weather	погода (ж)	[pa'gɔdə]
weather forecast	прогноз (м) погоды	[prag'nɔs pa'gɔdı]
temperature	температура (ж)	[timpera'tʊrə]
thermometer	термометр (м)	[tir'mɔmetr]
barometer	барометр (м)	[ba'rɔmetr]

humid (adj)	влажный	[v'laʒnıj]
humidity	влажность (ж)	[v'laʒnastʲ]
heat (extreme ~)	жара (ж)	[ʒa'ra]
hot (torrid)	жаркий	['ʒarkij]
it's hot	жарко	['ʒarkə]

| it's warm | тепло | [tip'lɔ] |
| warm (moderately hot) | тёплый | ['tɜplıj] |

| it's cold | холодно | ['hɔladnə] |
| cold (adj) | холодный | [ha'lɔdnıj] |

sun	солнце (с)	['sɔnʦe]
to shine (vi)	светить	[swi'titʲ]
sunny (day)	солнечный	['sɔlnitʃnıj]
to come up (vi)	взойти	[vzaj'ti]
to set (vi)	сесть	[sestʲ]

cloud	облако (с)	['ɔblakə]
cloudy (adj)	облачный	['ɔblatʃnıj]
rain cloud	туча (ж)	['tʊtʃə]
somber (gloomy)	пасмурный	['pasmʊrnıj]

rain	дождь (м)	[dɔʒtʲ]
it's raining	идёт дождь	[i'dɔt 'dɔʒtʲ]
rainy (~ day, weather)	дождливый	[daʒd'livıj]
to drizzle (vi)	моросить	[mara'sitʲ]
pouring rain	проливной дождь (м)	[praliv'nɔj dɔʒtʲ]

downpour	ливень (м)	['liweŋ]
heavy (e.g., ~ rain)	сильный	['silʌnɪj]
puddle	лужа (ж)	['luʒə]
to get wet (in rain)	промокнуть	[prɑ'mɔknutʲ]

fog (mist)	туман (м)	[tʊ'man]
foggy	туманный	[tʊ'mannɪj]
snow	снег (м)	[snek]
it's snowing	идёт снег	[i'dɜt s'nek]

86. Severe weather. Natural disasters

thunderstorm	гроза (ж)	[grɑ'za]
lightning (~ strike)	молния (ж)	['mɔlnija]
to flash (vi)	сверкать	[swir'katʲ]

thunder	гром (м)	[grɔm]
to thunder (vi)	греметь	[gri'metʲ]
it's thundering	гремит гром	[gri'mit grɔm]

| hail | град (м) | [grat] |
| it's hailing | идёт град | [i'dɜt g'rat] |

| to flood (vt) | затопить | [zatɑ'pitʲ] |
| flood, inundation | наводнение (с) | [navad'nenie] |

earthquake	землетрясение (с)	[zemletri'senie]
tremor, quake	толчок (м)	[tal'ʧɔk]
epicenter	эпицентр (м)	[ɛpi'ʦentr]
eruption	извержение (с)	[izwer'ʒɛnie]
lava	лава (ж)	['lavə]

twister	смерч (м)	[smertʃ]
tornado	торнадо (м)	[tar'nadə]
typhoon	тайфун (м)	[taj'fʊn]

hurricane	ураган (м)	[ura'gan]
storm	буря (ж)	['bʊrʲa]
tsunami	цунами (с)	[ʦu'nami]

cyclone	циклон (м)	[ʦɪk'lɔn]
bad weather	непогода (ж)	[nipa'gɔdə]
fire (accident)	пожар (м)	[pa'ʒar]
disaster	катастрофа (ж)	[katast'rɔfə]
meteorite	метеорит (м)	[mitea'rit]

avalanche	лавина (ж)	[la'winə]
snowslide	обвал (м)	[ab'val]
blizzard	метель (ж)	[mi'telʌ]
snowstorm	вьюга (ж)	['vjygə]

FAUNA

T&P Books Publishing

87. Mammals. Predators

predator	**хищник** (м)	['hiɕnik]
tiger	**тигр** (м)	[tigr]
lion	**лев** (м)	[lef]
wolf	**волк** (м)	[vɔlk]
fox	**лиса** (ж)	['lisə]
jaguar	**ягуар** (м)	[jagʊ'ɑr]
leopard	**леопард** (м)	[lia'pɑrt]
cheetah	**гепард** (м)	[gi'pɑrt]
black panther	**пантера** (ж)	[pan'tɛrə]
puma	**пума** (ж)	['pʊmə]
snow leopard	**снежный барс** (м)	[s'neʒnɪj bɑrs]
lynx	**рысь** (ж)	[rɪsʲ]
coyote	**койот** (м)	[ka'jot]
jackal	**шакал** (м)	[ʃʌ'kɑl]
hyena	**гиена** (ж)	[gi'enə]

88. Wild animals

animal	**животное** (с)	[ʒɪ'vɔtnɑe]
beast (animal)	**зверь** (м)	[zwerʲ]
squirrel	**белка** (ж)	['belkə]
hedgehog	**ёж** (м)	[ʒʃ]
hare	**заяц** (м)	['zaits]
rabbit	**кролик** (м)	[k'rɔlik]
badger	**барсук** (м)	[bar'sʊk]
raccoon	**енот** (м)	[e'nɔt]
hamster	**хомяк** (м)	[ha'mʲak]
marmot	**сурок** (м)	[sʊ'rɔk]
mole	**крот** (м)	[krɔt]
mouse	**мышь** (ж)	[mɪʃ]
rat	**крыса** (ж)	[k'rɪsə]
bat	**летучая мышь** (ж)	[le'tʊtʃija mɪʃ]
ermine	**горностай** (м)	[garnas'taj]
sable	**соболь** (м)	['sɔbaʎ]
marten	**куница** (ж)	[kʊ'nitsə]

| weasel | ласка (ж) | ['laskə] |
| mink | норка (ж) | ['nɔrkə] |

| beaver | бобр (м) | [bɔbr] |
| otter | выдра (ж) | ['vɪdrə] |

horse	лошадь (ж)	['lɔʃʌtʲ]
moose	лось (м)	[lɔsʲ]
deer	олень (м)	[a'leɲ]
camel	верблюд (м)	[wirb'lyt]

bison	бизон (м)	[bi'zɔn]
aurochs	зубр (м)	[zubr]
buffalo	буйвол (м)	['bʊjval]

zebra	зебра (ж)	['zebrə]
antelope	антилопа (ж)	[anti'lɔpə]
roe deer	косуля (ж)	[ka'sʊʎa]
fallow deer	лань (ж)	[laɲ]
chamois	серна (ж)	['sernə]
wild boar	кабан (м)	[ka'ban]

whale	кит (м)	[kit]
seal	тюлень (м)	[ty'leɲ]
walrus	морж (м)	[mɔrʃ]
fur seal	котик (м)	['kotik]
dolphin	дельфин (м)	[diʎ'fin]

bear	медведь (м)	[mid'wetʲ]
polar bear	белый медведь (м)	['belɪj mid'wetʲ]
panda	панда (ж)	['pandə]

monkey	обезьяна (ж)	[abi'zjanə]
chimpanzee	шимпанзе (с)	[ʃimpan'ze]
orangutan	орангутанг (м)	[arahgu'tank]
gorilla	горилла (ж)	[ga'rilə]
macaque	макака (ж)	[ma'kakə]
gibbon	гиббон (м)	[gi'bɔn]

| elephant | слон (м) | [slɔn] |
| rhinoceros | носорог (м) | [nasa'rɔk] |

| giraffe | жираф (м) | [ʒɪ'raf] |
| hippopotamus | бегемот (м) | [bige'mɔt] |

| kangaroo | кенгуру (м) | [kihgu'rʊ] |
| koala (bear) | коала (ж) | [ka'alə] |

mongoose	мангуст (м)	[ma'ɳust]
chinchilla	шиншилла (ж)	[ʃin'ʃilə]
skunk	скунс (м)	[skʊns]
porcupine	дикобраз (м)	[dikab'ras]

89. Domestic animals

| cat | кошка (ж) | ['kɔʃkə] |
| tomcat | кот (м) | [kɔt] |

horse	лошадь (ж)	['lɔʃʌtʲ]
stallion	жеребец (м)	[ʒɪre'bets]
mare	кобыла (ж)	[ka'bɪlə]

cow	корова (ж)	[ka'rɔvə]
bull	бык (м)	[bɪk]
ox	вол (м)	[vɔl]

sheep (ewe)	овца (ж)	[ɑv'tsa]
ram	баран (м)	[ba'rɑn]
goat	коза (ж)	[ka'za]
billy goat, he-goat	козёл (м)	[ka'zɜl]

| donkey | осёл (м) | [a'sɜl] |
| mule | мул (м) | [mʊl] |

pig, hog	свинья (ж)	[swi'ɲja]
piglet	поросёнок (м)	[para'sɜnak]
rabbit	кролик (м)	[k'rɔlik]

| hen (chicken) | курица (ж) | ['kʊritsə] |
| rooster | петух (м) | [pi'tʊh] |

duck	утка (ж)	['utkə]
drake	селезень (м)	['selezeɲ]
goose	гусь (м)	[gʊsʲ]

| tom turkey, gobbler | индюк (м) | [in'dyk] |
| turkey (hen) | индюшка (ж) | [in'dyʃkə] |

domestic animals	домашние животные (с мн)	[da'maʃnie ʒɪ'vɔtnie]
tame (e.g., ~ hamster)	ручной	[rʊtʲ'nɔj]
to tame (vt)	приручать	[prirʊ'tʃatʲ]
to breed (vt)	выращивать	[vɪ'raɕivatʲ]

farm	ферма (ж)	['fermə]
poultry	домашняя птица (ж)	[da'maʃnaja p'titsə]
cattle	скот (м)	[skɔt]
herd (cattle)	стадо (с)	[s'tadə]

stable	конюшня (ж)	[ka'nyʃɲa]
pigsty	свинарник (м)	[swi'narnik]
cowshed	коровник (м)	[ka'rɔvnik]
rabbit hutch	крольчатник (м)	[kraʎ'tʃatnik]
hen house	курятник (м)	[kʊ'rʲatnik]

90. Birds

bird	птица (ж)	[p'titsə]
pigeon	голубь (м)	['gɔlupʲ]
sparrow	воробей (м)	[vɑrɑ'bej]
tit	синица (ж)	[si'nitsə]
magpie	сорока (ж)	[sɑ'rɔkə]
raven	ворон (м)	['vɔrɑn]
crow	ворона (ж)	[vɑ'rɔnə]
jackdaw	галка (ж)	['gɑlkə]
rook	грач (м)	[grɑtʃ]
duck	утка (ж)	['utkə]
goose	гусь (м)	[gʊsʲ]
pheasant	фазан (м)	[fɑ'zɑn]
eagle	орёл (м)	[ɑ'rɜl]
hawk	ястреб (м)	['jastrep]
falcon	сокол (м)	['sɔkɑl]
vulture	гриф (м)	[grif]
condor (Andean ~)	кондор (м)	['kɔndɑr]
swan	лебедь (м)	['lebetʲ]
crane	журавль (м)	[ʒu'rɑvʌ]
stork	аист (м)	['ɑist]
parrot	попугай (м)	[pɑpʊ'gɑj]
hummingbird	колибри (ж)	[kɑ'libri]
peacock	павлин (м)	[pɑv'lin]
ostrich	страус (м)	[st'rɑus]
heron	цапля (ж)	['tsapʌa]
flamingo	фламинго (с)	[flɑ'mihgə]
pelican	пеликан (м)	[pili'kɑn]
nightingale	соловей (м)	[sɑlɑ'wej]
swallow	ласточка (ж)	['lɑstɑtʃkə]
thrush	дрозд (м)	[drɔzt]
song thrush	певчий дрозд (м)	['pevtʃij drɔzt]
blackbird	чёрный дрозд (м)	['tʃɔrnij drɔzt]
swift	стриж (м)	[striʃ]
lark	жаворонок (м)	['ʒavɑrɑnɑk]
quail	перепел (м)	['perepel]
woodpecker	дятел (м)	['dʲatel]
cuckoo	кукушка (ж)	[kʊ'kuʃkə]
owl	сова (ж)	[sɑ'va]
eagle owl	филин (м)	['filin]

wood grouse	глухарь (м)	[glu'harʲ]
black grouse	тетерев (м)	['teteref]
partridge	куропатка (ж)	[kʊra'patkə]

starling	скворец (м)	[skva'reʦ]
canary	канарейка (ж)	[kana'rejkə]
hazel grouse	рябчик (м)	['rʲabʧik]
chaffinch	зяблик (м)	['zʲablik]
bullfinch	снегирь (м)	[sni'girʲ]

seagull	чайка (ж)	['ʧajkə]
albatross	альбатрос (м)	[aʌbat'rɔs]
penguin	пингвин (м)	[pihg'win]

91. Fish. Marine animals

bream	лещ (м)	[leɕ]
carp	карп (м)	[karp]
perch	окунь (м)	['ɔkʊɲ]
catfish	сом (м)	[sɔm]
pike	щука (ж)	['ɕukə]

| salmon | лосось (м) | [la'sɔsʲ] |
| sturgeon | осётр (м) | [a'sɜtr] |

herring	сельдь (ж)	[seʌtʲ]
Atlantic salmon	сёмга (ж)	['sɜmgə]
mackerel	скумбрия (ж)	[s'kʊmbrija]
flatfish	камбала (ж)	['kambalə]

zander, pike perch	судак (м)	[sʊ'dak]
cod	треска (ж)	[tris'ka]
tuna	тунец (м)	[tʊ'neʦ]
trout	форель (ж)	[fa'reʌ]

eel	угорь (м)	['ugarʲ]
electric ray	электрический скат (м)	[ɛlekt'riʧeskij skat]
moray eel	мурена (ж)	[mʊ'renə]
piranha	пиранья (ж)	[pi'raɲja]

shark	акула (ж)	[a'kʊlə]
dolphin	дельфин (м)	[diʌ'fin]
whale	кит (м)	[kit]

crab	краб (м)	[krap]
jellyfish	медуза (ж)	[mi'dʊzə]
octopus	осьминог (м)	[asʲmi'nɔk]

| starfish | морская звезда (ж) | [mars'kaja zwez'da] |
| sea urchin | морской ёж (м) | [mars'kɔj ʒʃ] |

seahorse	морской конёк (м)	[mɑrs'kɔj kɑ'nɜk]
oyster	устрица (ж)	['ustritsə]
shrimp	креветка (ж)	[kri'wetkə]
lobster	омар (м)	[ɑ'mɑr]
spiny lobster	лангуст (м)	[lɑ'ŋust]

92. Amphibians. Reptiles

snake	змея (ж)	[zmi'ja]
venomous (snake)	ядовитый	[jɑdɑ'witɪj]
viper	гадюка (ж)	[gɑ'dykə]
cobra	кобра (ж)	['kɔbrə]
python	питон (м)	[pi'tɔn]
boa	удав (м)	[u'dɑf]
grass snake	уж (м)	[uʃ]
rattle snake	гремучая змея (ж)	[gri'mʊtʃaja zmi'ja]
anaconda	анаконда (ж)	[anɑ'kɔndə]
lizard	ящерица (ж)	['jaɕiritsə]
iguana	игуана (ж)	[igʊ'ɑnə]
monitor lizard	варан (м)	[vɑ'rɑn]
salamander	саламандра (ж)	[salɑ'mɑndrə]
chameleon	хамелеон (м)	[hɑmili'ɔn]
scorpion	скорпион (м)	[skɑrpi'ɔn]
turtle	черепаха (ж)	[tʃiri'pɑhə]
frog	лягушка (ж)	[li'gʊʃkə]
toad	жаба (ж)	['ʒɑbə]
crocodile	крокодил (м)	[krɑkɑ'dil]

93. Insects

insect, bug	насекомое (с)	[nase'kɔmɑe]
butterfly	бабочка (ж)	['bɑbɑtʃkə]
ant	муравей (м)	[mʊrɑ'wej]
fly	муха (ж)	['mʊhə]
mosquito	комар (м)	[kɑ'mɑr]
beetle	жук (м)	[ʒuk]
wasp	оса (ж)	[ɑ'sɑ]
bee	пчела (ж)	[ptʃi'lɑ]
bumblebee	шмель (м)	[ʃmeʎ]
gadfly	овод (м)	['ɔvɑt]
spider	паук (м)	[pɑ'uk]
spider's web	паутина (ж)	[pɑu'tinə]

dragonfly	стрекоза (ж)	[strekɑˈzɑ]
grasshopper	кузнечик (м)	[kʊzˈnetʃik]
moth (night butterfly)	мотылёк (м)	[mɑtɪˈlɜk]

cockroach	таракан (м)	[tɑrɑˈkɑn]
tick	клещ (м)	[kleɕ]
flea	блоха (ж)	[blɑˈhɑ]
midge	мошка (ж)	[ˈmɔʃkə]

locust	саранча (ж)	[sɑrɑɲˈtʃa]
snail	улитка (ж)	[uˈlitkə]
cricket	сверчок (м)	[swirˈtʃɔk]
lightning bug	светлячок (м)	[switliˈtʃɔk]
ladybug	божья коровка (ж)	[ˈbɔʒjɑ kɑˈrɔfkə]
cockchafer	майский жук (м)	[ˈmɑjskij ʒuk]

leech	пиявка (ж)	[piˈjafkə]
caterpillar	гусеница (ж)	[ˈgʊsenitsə]
earthworm	червь (м)	[ˈtʃerfʲ]
larva	личинка (ж)	[liˈtʃinkə]

FLORA

tree	**дерево** (с)	['derevə]
deciduous (adj)	**лиственное**	['listwenɑe]
coniferous (adj)	**хвойное**	[h'vɔjnɑe]
evergreen (adj)	**вечнозеленое**	[wetʃnaze'lɜnɑe]
apple tree	**яблоня** (ж)	['jablɑɲa]
pear tree	**груша** (ж)	[g'rʊʃə]
sweet cherry tree	**черешня** (ж)	[tʃi'reʃɲa]
sour cherry tree	**вишня** (ж)	['wiʃna]
plum tree	**слива** (ж)	[s'livə]
birch	**берёза** (ж)	[bi'rɜzə]
oak	**дуб** (м)	[dʊp]
linden tree	**липа** (ж)	['lipə]
aspen	**осина** (ж)	[ɑ'sinə]
maple	**клён** (м)	['klɜn]
spruce	**ель** (ж)	[eʎ]
pine	**сосна** (ж)	[sɑs'na]
larch	**лиственница** (ж)	['listwenitsə]
fir tree	**пихта** (ж)	['pihtə]
cedar	**кедр** (м)	[kedr]
poplar	**тополь** (м)	['tɔpɑʎ]
rowan	**рябина** (ж)	[ri'binə]
willow	**ива** (ж)	['ivə]
alder	**ольха** (ж)	[ɑʎ'ha]
beech	**бук** (м)	[bʊk]
elm	**вяз** (м)	[vʲas]
ash (tree)	**ясень** (м)	['jaseɲ]
chestnut	**каштан** (м)	[kaʃ'tan]
magnolia	**магнолия** (ж)	[mag'nɔlija]
palm tree	**пальма** (ж)	['paʎmə]
cypress	**кипарис** (м)	['kiparis]
mangrove	**мангровое дерево** (с)	['mɑhgravɑe 'derevə]
baobab	**баобаб** (м)	[bɑɑ'bap]
eucalyptus	**эвкалипт** (м)	[ɛfkɑ'lipt]
sequoia	**секвойя** (ж)	[sik'vɔja]

95. Shrubs

bush	куст (м)	[kʊst]
shrub	кустарник (м)	[kʊs'tarnik]
grapevine	виноград (м)	[winag'rat]
vineyard	виноградник (м)	[winag'radnik]
raspberry bush	малина (ж)	[ma'linə]
blackcurrant bush	чёрная смородина (ж)	['tʃɔrnaja sma'rɔdinə]
redcurrant bush	красная смородина (ж)	[k'rasnaja sma'rɔdinə]
gooseberry bush	крыжовник (м)	[krɪ'ʒɔvnik]
acacia	акация (ж)	[a'katsɪja]
barberry	барбарис (м)	[barba'ris]
jasmine	жасмин (м)	[ʒas'min]
juniper	можжевельник (м)	[maʒɛ'welʌnik]
rosebush	розовый куст (м)	['rɔzavɪj kʊst]
dog rose	шиповник (м)	[ʃɪ'pɔvnik]

96. Fruits. Berries

apple	яблоко (с)	['jablakə]
pear	груша (ж)	[g'rʊʃə]
plum	слива (ж)	[s'livə]
strawberry	клубника (ж)	[klub'nikə]
sour cherry	вишня (ж)	['wiʃna]
sweet cherry	черешня (ж)	[tʃɪ'reʃna]
grape	виноград (м)	[winag'rat]
raspberry	малина (ж)	[ma'linə]
blackcurrant	чёрная смородина (ж)	['tʃɔrnaja sma'rɔdinə]
redcurrant	красная смородина (ж)	[k'rasnaja sma'rɔdinə]
gooseberry	крыжовник (м)	[krɪ'ʒɔvnik]
cranberry	клюква (ж)	[k'lykvə]
orange	апельсин (м)	[apiʎ'sin]
mandarin	мандарин (м)	[manda'rin]
pineapple	ананас (м)	[ana'nas]
banana	банан (м)	[ba'nan]
date	финик (м)	['finik]
lemon	лимон (м)	[li'mɔn]
apricot	абрикос (м)	[abri'kɔs]
peach	персик (м)	['persik]
kiwi	киви (м)	['kiwi]
grapefruit	грейпфрут (м)	[gripf'rʊt]

berry	ягода (ж)	['jagədə]
berries	ягоды (ж мн)	['jagədɪ]
cowberry	брусника (ж)	[brʊs'nikə]
field strawberry	земляника (ж)	[zemli'nikə]
bilberry	черника (ж)	[tʃir'nikə]

97. Flowers. Plants

| flower | цветок (м) | [tswi'tɔk] |
| bouquet (of flowers) | букет (м) | [bʊ'ket] |

rose (flower)	роза (ж)	['rɔzə]
tulip	тюльпан (м)	[tyʌ'pan]
carnation	гвоздика (ж)	[gvaz'dikə]
gladiolus	гладиолус (м)	[gladi'ɔlus]

cornflower	василёк (м)	[vasi'lɜk]
bluebell	колокольчик (м)	[kala'kɔʌtʃik]
dandelion	одуванчик (м)	[adʊ'vaɲtʃik]
camomile	ромашка (ж)	[ra'maʃkə]

aloe	алоэ (с)	[a'lɔɛ]
cactus	кактус (м)	['kaktʊs]
rubber plant, ficus	фикус (м)	['fikʊs]

lily	лилия (ж)	['lilija]
geranium	герань (ж)	[gi'raɲ]
hyacinth	гиацинт (м)	[gia'tsɪnt]

mimosa	мимоза (ж)	[mi'mɔzə]
narcissus	нарцисс (м)	[nar'tsɪs]
nasturtium	настурция (ж)	[nas'tʊrtsija]

orchid	орхидея (ж)	[arhi'deja]
peony	пион (м)	[pi'ɔn]
violet	фиалка (ж)	[fi'alkə]

pansy	анютины глазки (мн)	[a'nytinɪ g'laski]
forget-me-not	незабудка (ж)	[niza'bʊtkə]
daisy	маргаритка (ж)	[marga'ritkə]

poppy	мак (м)	[mak]
hemp	конопля (ж)	[kanap'ʌa]
mint	мята (ж)	['mʲatə]

| lily of the valley | ландыш (м) | ['landɪʃ] |
| snowdrop | подснежник (м) | [pats'neʒnik] |

| nettle | крапива (ж) | [kra'pivə] |
| sorrel | щавель (м) | ['ɕaweʌ] |

water lily	кувшинка (ж)	[kuf'ʃinkə]
fern	папоротник (м)	['paparatnik]
lichen	лишайник (м)	[li'ʃʌjnik]

greenhouse (tropical ~)	оранжерея (ж)	[aranʒɪ'reja]
lawn	газон (м)	[ga'zɔn]
flowerbed	клумба (ж)	[k'lumbə]

plant	растение (с)	[ras'tenie]
grass	трава (ж)	[tra'va]
blade of grass	травинка (ж)	[tra'winkə]

leaf	лист (м)	[list]
petal	лепесток (м)	[lipes'tɔk]
stem	стебель (м)	[s'tebeʎ]
tuber	клубень (м)	[k'lubeɲ]

| young plant (shoot) | росток (м) | [ras'tɔk] |
| thorn | шип (м) | [ʃip] |

to blossom (vi)	цвести	[tswis'ti]
to fade, to wither	вянуть	['vʲanutʲ]
smell (odor)	запах (м)	['zapah]
to cut (flowers)	срезать	[s'rezatʲ]
to pick (a flower)	сорвать	[sar'vatʲ]

98. Cereals, grains

grain	зерно (с)	[zer'nɔ]
cereal crops	зерновые растения (с мн)	[zerna'vɪe ras'tenija]
ear (of barley, etc.)	колос (м)	['kɔlas]

wheat	пшеница (ж)	[pʃɪ'nitsə]
rye	рожь (ж)	[rɔʃ]
oats	овёс (м)	[a'wɜs]
millet	просо (с)	[p'rosə]
barley	ячмень (м)	[itʃʲ'meɲ]

corn	кукуруза (ж)	[kuku'ruzə]
rice	рис (м)	[ris]
buckwheat	гречиха (ж)	[gri'tʃihə]

pea plant	горох (м)	[ga'rɔh]
kidney bean	фасоль (ж)	[fa'sɔʎ]
soy	соя (ж)	['sɔja]
lentil	чечевица (ж)	[tʃitʃe'witsə]
beans (pulse crops)	бобы (мн)	[ba'bɪ]

BOOKS

T&P

COUNTRIES OF
THE WORLD

T&P Books Publishing

Afghanistan	Афганистан (м)	[afganis'tan]
Albania	Албания (ж)	[al'banija]
Argentina	Аргентина (ж)	[argen'tinə]
Armenia	Армения (ж)	[ar'menija]
Australia	Австралия (ж)	[afst'ralija]
Austria	Австрия (ж)	['afstrija]
Azerbaijan	Азербайджан (м)	[azirbaj'dʒan]
The Bahamas	Багамские острова (ж)	[ba'gamskie astra'va]
Bangladesh	Бангладеш (м)	[bahgla'deʃ]
Belarus	Беларусь (ж)	[bila'rusʲ]
Belgium	Бельгия (ж)	['beʎgija]
Bolivia	Боливия (ж)	[ba'liwija]
Bosnia and Herzegovina	Босния и Герцеговина (ж)	['bosnia i girʦəga'winə]
Brazil	Бразилия (ж)	[bra'zilija]
Bulgaria	Болгария (ж)	[bal'garija]
Cambodia	Камбоджа (ж)	[kam'bodʒə]
Canada	Канада (ж)	[ka'nadə]
Chile	Чили (ж)	['ʧili]
China	Китай (м)	[ki'taj]
Colombia	Колумбия (ж)	[ka'lumbija]
Croatia	Хорватия (ж)	[har'vatija]
Cuba	Куба (ж)	['kubə]
Cyprus	Кипр (м)	[kipr]
Czech Republic	Чехия (ж)	['ʧehija]
Denmark	Дания (ж)	['danija]
Dominican Republic	Доминиканская республика (ж)	[damini'kanskaja res'publikə]
Ecuador	Эквадор (м)	[ɛkva'dɔr]
Egypt	Египет (м)	[e'gipet]
England	Англия (ж)	['ahglija]
Estonia	Эстония (ж)	[ɛs'tonija]
Finland	Финляндия (ж)	[fin'ʎandija]
France	Франция (ж)	[f'ranʦɪja]
French Polynesia	Французская Полинезия (ж)	[fran'ʦuskaja pali'nezija]
Georgia	Грузия (ж)	[g'ruzija]
Germany	Германия (ж)	[gir'manija]
Ghana	Гана (ж)	['ganə]
Great Britain	Великобритания (ж)	[wilikabri'tanija]

Greece	Греция (ж)	[g'retsɪja]
Haiti	Гаити (м)	[gɑ'iti]
Hungary	Венгрия (ж)	['wehgrija]

100. Countries. Part 2

Iceland	Исландия (ж)	[is'landija]
India	Индия (ж)	['indija]
Indonesia	Индонезия (ж)	[indɑ'nɛzija]
Iran	Иран (м)	[i'ran]
Iraq	Ирак (м)	[i'rak]
Ireland	Ирландия (ж)	[ir'landija]
Israel	Израиль (м)	[iz'raiʎ]
Italy	Италия (ж)	[i'talija]

Jamaica	Ямайка (ж)	[ja'majkə]
Japan	Япония (ж)	[ja'pɔnija]
Jordan	Иордания (ж)	[iɑr'danija]
Kazakhstan	Казахстан (м)	[kazahs'tan]
Kenya	Кения (ж)	['kenija]
Kirghizia	Кыргызстан (м)	[kɪrgɪs'tan]
Kuwait	Кувейт (м)	[kʊ'wejt]

Laos	Лаос (м)	[la'ɔs]
Latvia	Латвия (ж)	['latwija]
Lebanon	Ливан (м)	[li'van]
Libya	Ливия (ж)	['liwija]
Liechtenstein	Лихтенштейн (м)	[lihtɛnʃ'tɛjn]
Lithuania	Литва (ж)	[lit'va]
Luxembourg	Люксембург (м)	[lyksem'bʊrk]

Macedonia (Republic of ~)	Македония (ж)	[make'dɔnija]
Madagascar	Мадагаскар (м)	[madagas'kar]
Malaysia	Малайзия (ж)	[ma'lajzija]
Malta	Мальта (ж)	['maʎtə]
Mexico	Мексика (ж)	['meksikə]
Moldova, Moldavia	Молдова (ж)	[mal'dɔvə]

Monaco	Монако (с)	[ma'nakə]
Mongolia	Монголия (ж)	[ma'ŋɔlija]
Montenegro	Черногория (ж)	[tʃirna'gɔrija]
Morocco	Марокко (с)	[ma'rɔkkə]
Myanmar	Мьянма (ж)	['mjanmə]

Namibia	Намибия (ж)	[na'mibija]
Nepal	Непал (м)	[ni'pal]
Netherlands	Нидерланды (мн)	[nider'landɪ]
New Zealand	Новая Зеландия (ж)	['nɔvaja ze'landija]
North Korea	Северная Корея (ж)	['sewernaja ka'reja]
Norway	Норвегия (ж)	[nar'wegija]

101. Countries. Part 3

Pakistan	Пакистан (м)	[pɑkisˈtɑn]
Palestine	Палестина (ж)	[pɑlesˈtinə]
Panama	Панама (ж)	[pɑˈnɑmə]
Paraguay	Парагвай (м)	[pɑrɑgˈvɑj]
Peru	Перу (с)	[piˈrʊ]
Poland	Польша (ж)	[ˈpɔʎʃə]
Portugal	Португалия (ж)	[pɑrtʊˈgɑlijɑ]
Romania	Румыния (ж)	[rʊˈmɪnijɑ]
Russia	Россия (ж)	[rɑˈsijɑ]

Saudi Arabia	Саудовская Аравия (ж)	[sɑˈudɑfskɑjɑ ɑˈrɑwijɑ]
Scotland	Шотландия (ж)	[ʃʌtˈlɑndijɑ]
Senegal	Сенегал (м)	[sineˈgɑl]
Serbia	Сербия (ж)	[ˈserbijɑ]
Slovakia	Словакия (ж)	[slɑˈvɑkijɑ]
Slovenia	Словения (ж)	[slɑˈwenijɑ]

South Africa	ЮАР (м)	[juˈɑr]
South Korea	Южная Корея (ж)	[ˈjuʒnɑjɑ kɑˈrejɑ]
Spain	Испания (ж)	[isˈpɑnijɑ]
Suriname	Суринам (м)	[sʊriˈnɑm]
Sweden	Швеция (ж)	[ʃˈwetsɪjɑ]
Switzerland	Швейцария (ж)	[ʃwiˈtsɑrijɑ]
Syria	Сирия (ж)	[ˈsirijɑ]

Taiwan	Тайвань (м)	[tɑjˈvɑɲ]
Tajikistan	Таджикистан (м)	[tɑdʒɪkisˈtɑn]
Tanzania	Танзания (ж)	[tɑnˈzɑnijɑ]
Tasmania	Тасмания (ж)	[tɑsˈmɑnijɑ]
Thailand	Таиланд (м)	[tɑiˈlɑnt]
Tunisia	Тунис (м)	[tʊˈnis]
Turkey	Турция (ж)	[ˈtʊrtsijɑ]
Turkmenistan	Туркменистан (м)	[tʊrkmenisˈtɑn]

Ukraine	Украина (ж)	[ukrɑˈinə]
United Arab Emirates	Объединённые Арабские Эмираты (мн)	[ɑbjediˈnɜnnɪe ɑˈrɑpskie ɛmiˈrɑtɪ]
United States of America	Соединённые Штаты (мн) Америки	[sɑediˈnɜnnɪe ʃˈtɑtɪ ɑˈmeriki]
Uruguay	Уругвай (м)	[urʊgˈvɑj]
Uzbekistan	Узбекистан (м)	[uzbekisˈtɑn]

Vatican	Ватикан (м)	[vɑtiˈkɑn]
Venezuela	Венесуэла (ж)	[winesʊˈɛlə]
Vietnam	Вьетнам (м)	[vjetˈnɑm]
Zanzibar	Занзибар (м)	[zɑnziˈbɑr]

GASTRONOMIC GLOSSARY

This section contains a lot of
words and terms associated
with food. This dictionary will
make it easier for you to
understand the menu at a
restaurant and choose
the right dish

T&P Books Publishing

aftertaste	привкус (м)	[p'rifkʊs]
almond	миндаль (м)	[min'daʎ]
anise	анис (м)	[a'nis]
aperitif	аперитив (м)	[apiri'tif]
appetite	аппетит (м)	[api'tit]
appetizer	закуска (ж)	[za'kʊskə]
apple	яблоко (с)	['jablakə]
apricot	абрикос (м)	[abri'kɔs]
artichoke	артишок (м)	[arti'ʃɔk]
asparagus	спаржа (ж)	[s'parʒə]
Atlantic salmon	сёмга (ж)	['sɜmgə]
avocado	авокадо (с)	[ava'kadə]
bacon	бекон (м)	[bi'kɔn]
banana	банан (м)	[ba'nan]
barley	ячмень (м)	[itʃ'menj]
bartender	бармен (м)	[bar'men]
basil	базилик (м)	[bazi'lik]
bay leaf	лавровый лист (м)	[lav'rɔvɪj list]
beans	бобы (мн)	[ba'bɪ]
beef	говядина (ж)	[ga'vʲadinə]
beer	пиво (с)	['pivə]
beetroot	свёкла (ж)	['swɜklə]
bell pepper	перец (м)	['perets]
berries	ягоды (ж мн)	['jagadɪ]
berry	ягода (ж)	['jagadə]
bilberry	черника (ж)	[tʃir'nikə]
birch bolete	подберёзовик (м)	[padbe'rzawik]
bitter	горький	['gɔrʲkij]
black coffee	чёрный кофе (м)	['tʃɔrnɪj 'kɔfe]
black pepper	чёрный перец (м)	['tʃɔrnɪj 'perets]
black tea	чёрный чай (м)	['tʃɔrnɪj tʃaj]
blackberry	ежевика (ж)	[eʒɪ'wikə]
blackcurrant	чёрная смородина (ж)	['tʃɔrnaja sma'rɔdinə]
boiled	варёный	[va'rɜnɪj]
bottle opener	открывалка (ж)	[atkrɪ'valkə]
bread	хлеб (м)	[hlep]
breakfast	завтрак (м)	['zaftrak]
bream	лещ (м)	[leɕ]
broccoli	капуста брокколи (ж)	[ka'pʊsta b'rɔkali]
Brussels sprouts	брюссельская капуста (ж)	[bry'seʎskaja ka'pʊstə]
buckwheat	гречиха (ж)	[gri'tʃihə]
butter	сливочное масло (с)	[s'livatʃnae 'maslə]
buttercream	крем (м)	[krem]

cabbage	капуста (ж)	[ka'pʊstə]
cake	пирожное (с)	[pi'rɔʒnae]
cake	торт (м)	[tɔrt]
calorie	калория (ж)	[ka'lɔrija]
can opener	открывалка (ж)	[atkrɪ'valkə]
candy	конфета (ж)	[kan'fetə]
canned food	консервы (мн)	[kan'servɪ]
cappuccino	кофе (м) со сливками	['kɔfe sɑ s'lifkami]
caraway	тмин (м)	[tmin]
carbohydrates	углеводы (мн)	[ugle'vɔdɪ]
carbonated	газированная	[gazi'rɔvanaja]
carp	карп (м)	[karp]
carrot	морковь (ж)	[mar'kɔfʲ]
catfish	сом (м)	[sɔm]
cauliflower	цветная капуста (ж)	[ʦwet'naja ka'pʊstə]
caviar	икра (ж)	[ik'ra]
celery	сельдерей (м)	[siʌde'rej]
cep	белый гриб (м)	['belɪj grip]
cereal crops	зерновые растения (с мн)	[zerna'vɪe ras'tenija]
cereal grains	крупа (ж)	[krʊ'pa]
champagne	шампанское (с)	[ʃʌm'panskae]
chanterelle	лисичка (ж)	[li'siʧkə]
check	счёт (м)	['ɕɜt]
cheese	сыр (м)	[sɪr]
chewing gum	жевательная резинка (м)	[ʒɪ'vateʌnaja re'zinkə]
chicken	курица (ж)	['kʊriʦə]
chocolate	шоколад (м)	[ʃʌka'lat]
chocolate	шоколадный	[ʃʌka'ladnɪj]
cinnamon	корица (ж)	[ka'riʦə]
clear soup	бульон (м)	[bʊ'ʎjon]
cloves	гвоздика (ж)	[gvaz'dikə]
cocktail	коктейль (м)	[kak'tɛjʌ]
coconut	кокосовый орех (м)	[ka'kɔsavɪj a'reh]
cod	треска (ж)	[tris'ka]
coffee	кофе (м)	['kɔfe]
coffee with milk	кофе (м) с молоком	['kɔfe s mala'kɔm]
cognac	коньяк (м)	[ka'ɲjak]
cold	холодный	[ha'lɔdnɪj]
condensed milk	сгущённое молоко (с)	[sgʊ'ɕɜnae mala'kɔ]
condiment	приправа (ж)	[prip'ravə]
confectionery	кондитерские изделия (мн)	[kan'diterskie iz'delija]
cookies	печенье (с)	[pi'ʧeɲje]
coriander	кориандр (м)	[kari'andr]
corkscrew	штопор (м)	[ʃ'tɔpar]
corn	кукуруза (ж)	[kʊkʊ'rʊzə]
corn	кукуруза (ж)	[kʊkʊ'rʊzə]
cornflakes	кукурузные хлопья (мн)	[kʊkʊ'rʊznɪe h'lɔpja]
course, dish	блюдо (с)	[b'lydə]
cowberry	брусника (ж)	[brʊs'nikə]

crab	краб (м)	[krap]
cranberry	клюква (ж)	[k'lykvə]
cream	сливки (мн)	[s'lifki]
crumb	крошка (ж)	[k'roʃkə]
crustaceans	ракообразные (мн)	[rakaab'raznıe]
cucumber	огурец (м)	[agʊ'rets]
cuisine	кухня (ж)	['kʊhɲa]
cup	чашка (ж)	['tʃaʃkə]
dark beer	тёмное пиво (с)	['tɜmnae 'pivə]
date	финик (м)	['finik]
death cap	поганка (ж)	[pa'gankə]
dessert	десерт (м)	[di'sert]
diet	диета (ж)	[di'etə]
dill	укроп (м)	[uk'rɔp]
dinner	ужин (м)	['uʒın]
dried	сушёный	[sʊ'ʃɔnıj]
drinking water	питьевая вода (ж)	[pitje'vaja va'da]
duck	утка (ж)	['utkə]
ear	колос (м)	['kɔlas]
edible mushroom	съедобный гриб (м)	[sʰe'dɔbnıj grip]
eel	угорь (м)	['ugarʲ]
egg	яйцо (с)	[jaj'tsɔ]
egg white	белок (м)	[bi'lɔk]
egg yolk	желток (м)	[ʒıl'tɔk]
eggplant	баклажан (м)	[bakla'ʒan]
eggs	яйца (мн)	['jajtsə]
Enjoy your meal!	Приятного аппетита!	[pri'jatnava ape'tita]
fats	жиры (мн)	[ʒı'rı]
field strawberry	земляника (ж)	[zemli'nikə]
fig	инжир (м)	[in'ʒir]
filling	начинка (ж)	[na'tʃinkə]
fish	рыба (ж)	['rıbə]
flatfish	камбала (ж)	['kambalə]
flour	мука (ж)	[mʊ'ka]
fly agaric	мухомор (м)	[mʊha'mɔr]
food	еда (ж)	[e'da]
fork	вилка (ж)	['wilkə]
freshly squeezed juice	свежевыжатый сок (м)	[sweʒɛ'vıʒatıj sɔk]
fried	жареный	['ʒarenıj]
fried eggs	яичница (ж)	[i'iʃnitsə]
fried meatballs	котлета (ж)	[kat'letə]
frozen	замороженный	[zama'rɔʒınıj]
fruit	фрукт (м)	[frʊkt]
game	дичь (ж)	[ditʃ]
gammon	окорок (м)	['ɔkarak]
garlic	чеснок (м)	[tʃis'nɔk]
gin	джин (м)	[dʒın]
ginger	имбирь (м)	[im'birʲ]
glass	стакан (м)	[sta'kan]
glass	бокал (м)	[ba'kal]
goose	гусь (м)	[gʊsʲ]
gooseberry	крыжовник (м)	[krı'ʒɔvnik]

grain	зерно (c)	[zer'nɔ]
grape	виноград (м)	[winag'rat]
grapefruit	грейпфрут (м)	[gripf'rʊt]
green tea	зелёный чай (м)	[ziʲlɜnɪj ʧaj]
greens	зелень (ж)	['zelɛɲ]
halibut	палтус (м)	['paltʊs]
ham	ветчина (ж)	[witʃi'na]
hamburger	фарш (м)	[farʃ]
hamburger	гамбургер (м)	['gambʊrger]
hazelnut	лесной орех (м)	[lis'nɔj a'reh]
herring	сельдь (ж)	[seʌtʲ]
honey	мёд (м)	['mɜt]
horseradish	хрен (м)	[hren]
hot	горячий	[ga'rʲatʃij]
ice	лёд (м)	['lɜt]
ice-cream	мороженое (c)	[ma'rɔʒnae]
instant coffee	растворимый кофе (м)	[rastva'rimɪj 'kɔfe]
jam	джем, конфитюр	[dʒɛm], [kanfi'tyr]
jam	варенье (c)	[va'reɲje]
juice	сок (м)	[sɔk]
kidney bean	фасоль (ж)	[fa'sɔʌ]
kiwi	киви (м)	['kiwi]
knife	нож (м)	[nɔʃ]
lamb	баранина (ж)	[ba'raninə]
lard	сало (c)	['salə]
lemon	лимон (м)	[li'mɔn]
lemonade	лимонад (м)	[lima'nat]
lentil	чечевица (ж)	[ʧiʧe'witsə]
lettuce	салат (м)	[sa'lat]
light beer	светлое пиво (c)	[s'wetlae 'pivə]
liqueur	ликёр (м)	[li'kɜr]
liquors	алкогольные напитки (мн)	[alka'gɔʌnɪe na'pitki]
liver	печень (ж)	['petʃeɲ]
lunch	обед (м)	[a'bet]
mackerel	скумбрия (ж)	[s'kʊmbrija]
mandarin	мандарин (м)	[manda'rin]
mango	манго (c)	['mahgə]
margarine	маргарин (м)	[marga'rin]
marmalade	мармелад (м)	[marme'lat]
mashed potatoes	картофельное пюре (c)	[kar'tɔfeʌnae py'rɛ]
mayonnaise	майонез (м)	[mai'nɛs]
meat	мясо (c)	['mʲase]
melon	дыня (ж)	['dɪɲa]
menu	меню (c)	[mi'ny]
milk	молоко (c)	[mala'kɔ]
milkshake	молочный коктейль (м)	[ma'lɔtʃnɪj kak'tɛjʌ]
millet	просо (c)	[p'rɔsə]
mineral water	минеральная вода (ж)	[mini'raʌnaja va'da]
morel	сморчок (м)	[smar'ʧɔk]
mushroom	гриб (м)	[grip]
mustard	горчица (ж)	[gar'ʧitsə]

non-alcoholic	безалкогольный	[bizalka'gɔʌnɪj]
noodles	лапша (ж)	[lap'ʃʌ]
oats	овёс (м)	[a'wɜs]
olive oil	оливковое масло (с)	[a'lifkavae 'maslə]
olives	оливки (мн)	[a'lifki]
omelet	омлет (м)	[am'let]
onion	лук (м)	[luk]
orange	апельсин (м)	[apiʌ'sin]
orange juice	апельсиновый сок (м)	[apiʌ'sinavɪj sɔk]
orange-cap boletus	подосиновик (м)	[pada'sinawik]
oyster	устрица (ж)	['ustritsə]
pâté	паштет (м)	[paʃ'tet]
papaya	папайя (ж)	[pa'paja]
paprika	паприка (ж)	['paprikə]
parsley	петрушка (ж)	[pit'ruʃkə]
pasta	макароны (мн)	[maka'rɔnɪ]
pea	горох (м)	[ga'rɔh]
peach	персик (м)	['persik]
peanut	арахис (м)	[a'rahis]
pear	груша (ж)	[g'ruʃə]
peel	кожура (ж)	[kaʒu'ra]
perch	окунь (м)	['ɔkʊɲ]
pickled	маринованный	[mari'nɔvanɪj]
pie	пирог (м)	[pi'rɔk]
piece	кусок (м)	[kʊ'sɔk]
pike	щука (ж)	['ɕukə]
pike perch	судак (м)	[sʊ'dak]
pineapple	ананас (м)	[ana'nas]
pistachios	фисташки (мн)	[fis'taʃki]
pizza	пицца (ж)	['pitsə]
plate	тарелка (ж)	[ta'relkə]
plum	слива (ж)	[s'livə]
poisonous mushroom	ядовитый гриб (м)	[jada'witɪj grip]
pomegranate	гранат (м)	[gra'nat]
pork	свинина (ж)	[swi'ninə]
porridge	каша (ж)	['kaʃə]
portion	порция (ж)	['pɔrtsɪja]
potato	картофель (м)	[kar'tɔfeʌ]
proteins	белки (мн)	[bil'ki]
pub, bar	бар (м)	[bar]
pudding	пудинг (м)	['pʊdink]
pumpkin	тыква (ж)	['tɪkvə]
rabbit	кролик (м)	[k'rɔlik]
radish	редис (м)	[ri'dis]
raisin	изюм (м)	[i'zym]
raspberry	малина (ж)	[ma'linə]
recipe	рецепт (м)	[ri'tsəpt]
red pepper	красный перец (м)	[k'rasnɪj 'perets]
red wine	красное вино (с)	[k'rasnae wi'nɔ]
redcurrant	красная смородина (ж)	[k'rasnaja sma'rɔdinə]
refreshing drink	прохладительный напиток (м)	[prahla'diteʌnɪj na'pitak]

rice	рис (м)	[ris]
rum	ром (м)	[rom]
russula	сыроежка (ж)	[sɪrɑˈeʃkə]
rye	рожь (ж)	[rɔʃ]
saffron	шафран (м)	[ʃʌfˈran]
salad	салат (м)	[sɑˈlat]
salmon	лосось (м)	[lɑˈsɔsʲ]
salt	соль (ж)	[sɔʎ]
salty	солёный	[sɑˈlɜnɪj]
sandwich	бутерброд (м)	[bʊterbˈrɔt]
sardine	сардина (ж)	[sɑrˈdinə]
sauce	соус (м)	[ˈsɔus]
saucer	блюдце (с)	[bˈlʲutse]
sausage	колбаса (ж)	[kɑlbɑˈsɑ]
seafood	морепродукты (мн)	[mɑreprɑˈdʊktɪ]
sesame	кунжут (м)	[kʊnˈʒut]
shark	акула (ж)	[ɑˈkʊlə]
shrimp	креветка (ж)	[kriˈwetkə]
side dish	гарнир (м)	[gɑrˈnir]
slice	ломтик (м)	[ˈlɔmtik]
smoked	копчёный	[kɑpˈʧɔnɪj]
soft drink	безалкогольный напиток (м)	[bizɑlkɑˈgɔʎnɪj nɑˈpitɑk]
soup	суп (м)	[sʊp]
soup spoon	столовая ложка (ж)	[stɑˈlɔvɑjɑ ˈlɔʃkə]
sour cherry	вишня (ж)	[ˈwiʃnɑ]
sour cream	сметана (ж)	[smiˈtɑnə]
soy	соя (ж)	[ˈsɔjɑ]
spaghetti	спагетти (мн)	[spɑˈgetti]
sparkling	с газом	[s gɑzɑm]
spice	пряность (ж)	[pˈrʲanɑstʲ]
spinach	шпинат (м)	[ʃpiˈnat]
spiny lobster	лангуст (м)	[lɑˈŋust]
spoon	ложка (ж)	[ˈlɔʃkə]
squid	кальмар (м)	[kɑʎˈmɑr]
steak	бифштекс (м)	[bifʃˈtɛks]
stew	жаркое (с)	[ʒɑrˈkɔe]
still	без газа	[bez ˈgɑzə]
strawberry	клубника (ж)	[klubˈnikə]
sturgeon	осетрина (ж)	[ɑsitˈrinə]
sugar	сахар (м)	[ˈsɑhɑr]
sunflower oil	подсолнечное масло (с)	[pɑˈtsɔlnetʃnɑe ˈmaslə]
sweet	сладкий	[sˈlatkij]
sweet cherry	черешня (ж)	[ʧiˈreʃnɑ]
taste, flavor	вкус (м)	[fkʊs]
tasty	вкусный	[fˈkʊsnɪj]
tea	чай (м)	[ʧaj]
teaspoon	чайная ложка (ж)	[ˈʧajnɑjɑ ˈlɔʃkə]
tip	чаевые (мн)	[ʧiiˈvie]
tomato	помидор (м)	[pɑmiˈdɔr]
tomato juice	томатный сок (м)	[tɑˈmatnɪj sɔk]
tongue	язык (м)	[jɑˈzɪk]

toothpick	зубочистка (ж)	[zuba'tʃistkə]
trout	форель (ж)	[fa'reʎ]
tuna	тунец (м)	[tʊ'nets]
turkey	индейка (ж)	[in'dejkə]
turnip	репа (ж)	['repə]
veal	телятина (ж)	[ti'ʎatinə]
vegetable oil	растительное масло (с)	[ras'titeʎnae 'maslə]
vegetables	овощи (м мн)	['ɔvaɕi]
vegetarian	вегетарианец (м)	[wigitari'anets]
vegetarian	вегетарианский	[wigitari'anskij]
vermouth	вермут (м)	['wermʊt]
vienna sausage	сосиска (ж)	[sa'siskə]
vinegar	уксус (м)	['uksʊs]
vitamin	витамин (м)	[wita'min]
vodka	водка (ж)	['vɔtkə]
waffles	вафли (мн)	['vafli]
waiter	официант (м)	[afitsɪ'ant]
waitress	официантка (ж)	[afitsɪ'antkə]
walnut	грецкий орех (м)	[g'retskij a'reh]
water	вода (ж)	[va'da]
watermelon	арбуз (м)	[ar'bʊs]
wheat	пшеница (ж)	[pʃɪ'nitsə]
whisky	виски (с)	['wiski]
white wine	белое вино (с)	['belae wi'nɔ]
wine	вино (с)	[wi'nɔ]
wine list	карта (ж) вин	['karta win]
with ice	со льдом	[saʎ'dɔm]
yogurt	йогурт (м)	['jogʊrt]
zucchini	кабачок (м)	[kaba'tʃɔk]

абрикос (м)	[abri'kɔs]	apricot
авокадо (с)	[ava'kadə]	avocado
акула (ж)	[a'kʊlə]	shark
алкогольные напитки (мн)	[alka'gоʌnıe na'pitki]	liquors
ананас (м)	[ana'nas]	pineapple
анис (м)	[a'nis]	anise
апельсин (м)	[apiʎ'sin]	orange
апельсиновый сок (м)	[apiʎ'sinavıj sɔk]	orange juice
аперитив (м)	[apiri'tif]	aperitif
аппетит (м)	[api'tit]	appetite
арахис (м)	[a'rahis]	peanut
арбуз (м)	[ar'bʊs]	watermelon
артишок (м)	[arti'ʃɔk]	artichoke
базилик (м)	[bazi'lik]	basil
баклажан (м)	[bakla'ʒan]	eggplant
банан (м)	[ba'nan]	banana
бар (м)	[bar]	pub, bar
баранина (ж)	[ba'raninə]	lamb
бармен (м)	[bar'men]	bartender
без газа	[bez 'gazə]	still
безалкогольный	[bizalka'gɔʌnıj]	non-alcoholic
безалкогольный напиток (м)	[bizalka'gɔʌnıj na'pitak]	soft drink
бекон (м)	[bi'kɔn]	bacon
белки (мн)	[bil'ki]	proteins
белое вино (с)	['belae wi'nɔ]	white wine
белок (м)	[bi'lɔk]	egg white
белый гриб (м)	['belıj grip]	cep
бифштекс (м)	[bifʃ'tɛks]	steak
блюдо (с)	[b'lydə]	course, dish
блюдце (с)	[b'lytsе]	saucer
бобы (мн)	[ba'bı]	beans
бокал (м)	[ba'kal]	glass
брусника (ж)	[brʊs'nikə]	cowberry
брюссельская капуста (ж)	[bry'seʌskaja ka'pʊstə]	Brussels sprouts
бульон (м)	[bʊ'ʎjon]	clear soup
бутерброд (м)	[bʊterb'rɔt]	sandwich
варенье (с)	[va'renje]	jam
варёный	[va'rɜnıj]	boiled
вафли (мн)	['vafli]	waffles
вегетарианец (м)	[wigitari'anets]	vegetarian
вегетарианский	[wigitari'anskij]	vegetarian

вермут (м)	['wermʊt]	vermouth
ветчина (ж)	[witʃi'na]	ham
вилка (ж)	['wilkə]	fork
вино (с)	[wi'nɔ]	wine
виноград (м)	[winag'rat]	grape
виски (с)	['wiski]	whisky
витамин (м)	[wita'min]	vitamin
вишня (ж)	['wiʃna]	sour cherry
вкус (м)	[fkʊs]	taste, flavor
вкусный	[f'kʊsnɪj]	tasty
вода (ж)	[va'da]	water
водка (ж)	['vɔtkə]	vodka
газированная	[gazi'rɔvanaja]	carbonated
гамбургер (м)	['gambʊrger]	hamburger
гарнир (м)	[gar'nir]	side dish
гвоздика (ж)	[gvaz'dikə]	cloves
говядина (ж)	[ga'vʲadinə]	beef
горох (м)	[ga'rɔh]	pea
горчица (ж)	[gar'tʃitsə]	mustard
горький	['gorʲkij]	bitter
горячий	[ga'rʲatʃij]	hot
гранат (м)	[gra'nat]	pomegranate
грейпфрут (м)	[gripf'rʊt]	grapefruit
грецкий орех (м)	[g'retskij a'reh]	walnut
гречиха (ж)	[gri'tʃihə]	buckwheat
гриб (м)	[grip]	mushroom
груша (ж)	[g'rʊʃə]	pear
гусь (м)	[gʊsʲ]	goose
десерт (м)	[di'sert]	dessert
джем, конфитюр	[dʒɛm], [kanfi'tyr]	jam
джин (м)	[dʒɪn]	gin
диета (ж)	[di'etə]	diet
дичь (ж)	[ditʃ]	game
дыня (ж)	['dɪɲa]	melon
еда (ж)	[e'da]	food
ежевика (ж)	[eʒɪ'wikə]	blackberry
жареный	['ʒarenɪj]	fried
жаркое (с)	[ʒar'kɔe]	stew
жевательная резинка (м)	[ʒɪ'vateʎnaja re'zinkə]	chewing gum
желток (м)	[ʒɪl'tɔk]	egg yolk
жиры (мн)	[ʒɪ'rɪ]	fats
завтрак (м)	['zaftrak]	breakfast
закуска (ж)	[za'kʊskə]	appetizer
замороженный	[zama'rɔʒɪnɪj]	frozen
зелень (ж)	['zeleɲ]	greens
зелёный чай (м)	[zi'lɔnɪj tʃaj]	green tea
земляника (ж)	[zemli'nikə]	field strawberry
зерно (с)	[zer'nɔ]	grain
зерновые растения (с мн)	[zerna'vʲie ras'tenija]	cereal crops
зубочистка (ж)	[zuba'tʃistkə]	toothpick

изюм (м)	[i'zym]	raisin
икра (ж)	[ik'ra]	caviar
имбирь (м)	[im'bir']	ginger
индейка (ж)	[in'dejkə]	turkey
инжир (м)	[in'ʒir]	fig
йогурт (м)	['jogʊrt]	yogurt
кабачок (м)	[kaba'ʧɔk]	zucchini
калория (ж)	[ka'lɔrija]	calorie
кальмар (м)	[kaʎ'mar]	squid
камбала (ж)	['kambalə]	flatfish
капуста (ж)	[ka'pʊstə]	cabbage
капуста брокколи (ж)	[ka'pʊstə b'rɔkali]	broccoli
карп (м)	[karp]	carp
карта (ж) вин	['karta win]	wine list
картофель (м)	[kar'tɔfeʎ]	potato
картофельное пюре (с)	[kar'tɔfeʎnae py'rɛ]	mashed potatoes
каша (ж)	['kaʃə]	porridge
киви (м)	['kiwi]	kiwi
клубника (ж)	[klub'nikə]	strawberry
клюква (ж)	[k'lykvə]	cranberry
кожура (ж)	[kaʒu'ra]	peel
кокосовый орех (м)	[ka'kɔsavij a'reh]	coconut
коктейль (м)	[kak'tɛjʎ]	cocktail
колбаса (ж)	[kalba'sa]	sausage
колос (м)	['kɔlas]	ear
кондитерские изделия (мн)	[kan'diterskie iz'delija]	confectionery
консервы (мн)	[kan'servɪ]	canned food
конфета (ж)	[kan'fetə]	candy
коньяк (м)	[ka'njak]	cognac
копчёный	[kap'ʧɔnɪj]	smoked
кориандр (м)	[kari'andr]	coriander
корица (ж)	[ka'ritsə]	cinnamon
котлета (ж)	[kat'letə]	fried meatballs
кофе (м)	['kɔfe]	coffee
кофе (м) с молоком	['kɔfe s mala'kɔm]	coffee with milk
кофе (м) со сливками	['kɔfe sa s'lifkami]	cappuccino
краб (м)	[krap]	crab
красная смородина (ж)	[k'rasnaja sma'rɔdinə]	redcurrant
красное вино (с)	[k'rasnae wi'nɔ]	red wine
красный перец (м)	[k'rasnɪj 'perets]	red pepper
креветка (ж)	[kri'wetkə]	shrimp
крем (м)	[krem]	buttercream
кролик (м)	[k'rɔlik]	rabbit
крошка (ж)	[k'rɔʃkə]	crumb
крупа (ж)	[krʊ'pa]	cereal grains
крыжовник (м)	[krɪ'ʒovnik]	gooseberry
кукуруза (ж)	[kʊkʊ'rʊzə]	corn
кукуруза (ж)	[kʊkʊ'rʊzə]	corn
кукурузные хлопья (мн)	[kʊkʊ'rʊznɪe h'lɔpja]	cornflakes
кунжут (м)	[kʊn'ʒut]	sesame
курица (ж)	['kʊritsə]	chicken

кусок (м)	[kʊ'sɔk]	piece
кухня (ж)	['kʊhɲɑ]	cuisine
лавровый лист (м)	[lɑv'rɔvɪj list]	bay leaf
лангуст (м)	[lɑ'ŋust]	spiny lobster
лапша (ж)	[lɑp'ʃʌ]	noodles
лесной орех (м)	[lis'nɔj ɑ'reh]	hazelnut
лещ (м)	[leɕ]	bream
лёд (м)	['lɜt]	ice
ликёр (м)	[li'kɜr]	liqueur
лимон (м)	[li'mɔn]	lemon
лимонад (м)	[limɑ'nɑt]	lemonade
лисичка (ж)	[li'sitʃkə]	chanterelle
ложка (ж)	['lɔʃkə]	spoon
ломтик (м)	['lɔmtik]	slice
лосось (м)	[lɑ'sɔsʲ]	salmon
лук (м)	[luk]	onion
майонез (м)	[mai'nɛs]	mayonnaise
макароны (мн)	[makɑ'rɔnɪ]	pasta
малина (ж)	[mɑ'linə]	raspberry
манго (с)	['mɑhɡə]	mango
мандарин (м)	[mandɑ'rin]	mandarin
маргарин (м)	[mɑrɡɑ'rin]	margarine
маринованный	[mɑri'nɔvɑnɪj]	pickled
мармелад (м)	[mɑrme'lɑt]	marmalade
меню (с)	[mi'ny]	menu
мёд (м)	['mɜt]	honey
миндаль (м)	[min'dɑʎ]	almond
минеральная вода (ж)	[mini'rɑʎnɑjɑ vɑ'dɑ]	mineral water
молоко (с)	[mɑlɑ'kɔ]	milk
молочный коктейль (м)	[mɑ'lɔtʃnɪj kɑk'tɛjʎ]	milkshake
морепродукты (мн)	[mɑreprɑ'dʊktɪ]	seafood
морковь (ж)	[mɑr'kɔfʲ]	carrot
мороженое (с)	[mɑ'rɔʒnɑe]	ice-cream
мука (ж)	[mʊ'kɑ]	flour
мухомор (м)	[mʊhɑ'mɔr]	fly agaric
мясо (с)	['mʲɑsə]	meat
начинка (ж)	[nɑ'tʃinkə]	filling
нож (м)	[nɔʃ]	knife
обед (м)	[ɑ'bet]	lunch
овёс (м)	[ɑ'wɜs]	oats
овощи (м мн)	['ɔvɑɕi]	vegetables
огурец (м)	[aɡʊ'rets]	cucumber
окорок (м)	['ɔkɑrɑk]	gammon
окунь (м)	['ɔkʊɲ]	perch
оливки (мн)	[ɑ'lifki]	olives
оливковое масло (с)	[ɑ'lifkɑvɑe 'mɑslə]	olive oil
омлет (м)	[ɑm'let]	omelet
осетрина (ж)	[ɑsit'rinə]	sturgeon
открывалка (ж)	[ɑtkrɪ'vɑlkə]	bottle opener
открывалка (ж)	[ɑtkrɪ'vɑlkə]	can opener
официант (м)	[ɑfitsɪ'ɑnt]	waiter
официантка (ж)	[ɑfitsɪ'ɑntkə]	waitress

палтус (м)	['paltʊs]	halibut
папайя (ж)	[pa'paja]	papaya
паприка (ж)	['paprikə]	paprika
паштет (м)	[paʃ'tet]	pâté
перец (м)	['perets]	bell pepper
персик (м)	['persik]	peach
петрушка (ж)	[pit'rʊʃkə]	parsley
печень (ж)	['petʃeɲ]	liver
печенье (с)	[pi'tʃeɲje]	cookies
пиво (с)	['pivə]	beer
пирог (м)	[pi'rɔk]	pie
пирожное (с)	[pi'rɔʒnɑe]	cake
питьевая вода (ж)	[pitje'vaja va'da]	drinking water
пицца (ж)	['pitsə]	pizza
поганка (ж)	[pa'gankə]	death cap
подберёзовик (м)	[padbe'rzawik]	birch bolete
подосиновик (м)	[pada'sinawik]	orange-cap boletus
подсолнечное масло (с)	[pa'tsɔlnetʃnae 'maslə]	sunflower oil
помидор (м)	[pami'dɔr]	tomato
порция (ж)	['pɔrtsɪja]	portion
привкус (м)	[p'rifkʊs]	aftertaste
приправа (ж)	[prip'ravə]	condiment
Приятного аппетита!	[pri'jatnava ape'tita]	Enjoy your meal!
просо (с)	[p'rɔsə]	millet
прохладительный напиток (м)	[prahla'diteʌnɪj na'pitak]	refreshing drink
пряность (ж)	[p'rʲanastʲ]	spice
пудинг (м)	['pʊdink]	pudding
пшеница (ж)	[pʃɪ'nitsə]	wheat
ракообразные (мн)	[rakaab'raznɪe]	crustaceans
растворимый кофе (м)	[rastva'rimɪj 'kɔfe]	instant coffee
растительное масло (с)	[ras'titeʌnae 'maslə]	vegetable oil
редис (м)	[ri'dis]	radish
репа (ж)	['repə]	turnip
рецепт (м)	[ri'tsəpt]	recipe
рис (м)	[ris]	rice
рожь (ж)	[rɔʃ]	rye
ром (м)	[rɔm]	rum
рыба (ж)	['rɪbə]	fish
с газом	[s gazam]	sparkling
салат (м)	[sɑ'lat]	lettuce
салат (м)	[sɑ'lat]	salad
сало (с)	['salə]	lard
сардина (ж)	[sar'dinə]	sardine
сахар (м)	['sahar]	sugar
свежевыжатый сок (м)	[sweʒɛ'vɪʒatɪj sɔk]	freshly squeezed juice
светлое пиво (с)	[s'wetlae 'pivə]	light beer
свёкла (ж)	['swɜklə]	beetroot
свинина (ж)	[swi'ninə]	pork
сгущённое молоко (с)	[sgʊ'ɕɜnae mala'kɔ]	condensed milk
сельдерей (м)	[siʌde'rej]	celery
сельдь (ж)	[seʌtʲ]	herring

сёмга (ж)	[ˈsɜmgə]	Atlantic salmon
скумбрия (ж)	[sˈkumbrijа]	mackerel
сладкий	[sˈlatkij]	sweet
слива (ж)	[sˈlivə]	plum
сливки (мн)	[sˈlifki]	cream
сливочное масло (с)	[sˈlivatʃnае ˈmaslə]	butter
сметана (ж)	[smiˈtanə]	sour cream
сморчок (м)	[smarˈtʃɔk]	morel
со льдом	[saʎˈdom]	with ice
сок (м)	[sɔk]	juice
солёный	[saˈlɜnɪj]	salty
соль (ж)	[sɔʎ]	salt
сом (м)	[sɔm]	catfish
сосиска (ж)	[saˈsiskə]	vienna sausage
соус (м)	[ˈsоus]	sauce
соя (ж)	[ˈsɔjа]	soy
спагетти (мн)	[spaˈgetti]	spaghetti
спаржа (ж)	[sˈparʒə]	asparagus
стакан (м)	[staˈkan]	glass
столовая ложка (ж)	[staˈlovaja ˈlɔʃkə]	soup spoon
судак (м)	[suˈdak]	pike perch
суп (м)	[sup]	soup
сушёный	[suˈʃɔnɪj]	dried
счёт (м)	[ˈɕɜt]	check
съедобный гриб (м)	[sʰeˈdɔbnɪj grip]	edible mushroom
сыр (м)	[sɪr]	cheese
сыроежка (ж)	[sɪraˈeʃkə]	russula
тарелка (ж)	[taˈrelkə]	plate
телятина (ж)	[tiˈʎatinə]	veal
тёмное пиво (с)	[ˈtɜmnае ˈpivə]	dark beer
тмин (м)	[tmin]	caraway
томатный сок (м)	[taˈmatnɪj sɔk]	tomato juice
торт (м)	[tɔrt]	cake
треска (ж)	[trisˈka]	cod
тунец (м)	[tuˈnets]	tuna
тыква (ж)	[ˈtɪkvə]	pumpkin
углеводы (мн)	[ugleˈvodɪ]	carbohydrates
угорь (м)	[ˈugarʲ]	eel
ужин (м)	[ˈuʒɪn]	dinner
укроп (м)	[ukˈrɔp]	dill
уксус (м)	[ˈuksus]	vinegar
устрица (ж)	[ˈustritsə]	oyster
утка (ж)	[ˈutkə]	duck
фарш (м)	[farʃ]	hamburger
фасоль (ж)	[faˈsɔʎ]	kidney bean
финик (м)	[ˈfinik]	date
фисташки (мн)	[fisˈtaʃki]	pistachios
форель (ж)	[faˈreʎ]	trout
фрукт (м)	[frukt]	fruit
хлеб (м)	[hlep]	bread
холодный	[haˈlodnɪj]	cold
хрен (м)	[hren]	horseradish

цветная капуста (ж)	[tsvet'naja ka'pustə]	cauliflower
чаевые (мн)	[tʃii'vɪe]	tip
чай (м)	[tʃaj]	tea
чайная ложка (ж)	['tʃajnaja 'loʃkə]	teaspoon
чашка (ж)	['tʃaʃkə]	cup
черешня (ж)	[tʃi'reʃna]	sweet cherry
черника (ж)	[tʃir'nikə]	bilberry
чеснок (м)	[tʃis'nɔk]	garlic
чечевица (ж)	[tʃitʃe'witsə]	lentil
чёрная смородина (ж)	['tʃornaja sma'rɔdinə]	blackcurrant
чёрный кофе (м)	['tʃornɪj 'kofe]	black coffee
чёрный перец (м)	['tʃornɪj 'perets]	black pepper
чёрный чай (м)	['tʃornɪj tʃaj]	black tea
шампанское (с)	[ʃʌm'panskae]	champagne
шафран (м)	[ʃʌf'ran]	saffron
шоколад (м)	[ʃʌka'lat]	chocolate
шоколадный	[ʃʌka'ladnɪj]	chocolate
шпинат (м)	[ʃpi'nat]	spinach
штопор (м)	[ʃ'topar]	corkscrew
щука (ж)	['ɕukə]	pike
яблоко (с)	['jablakə]	apple
ягода (ж)	['jagadə]	berry
ягоды (ж мн)	['jagadɪ]	berries
ядовитый гриб (м)	[jada'witɪj grip]	poisonous mushroom
язык (м)	[ja'zɪk]	tongue
яичница (ж)	[i'iʃnitsə]	fried eggs
яйца (мн)	['jajtsə]	eggs
яйцо (с)	[jaj'tsɔ]	egg
ячмень (м)	[itʃ'meɲ]	barley